OF SHIPS AND MEN

OF SHIPS AND MEN

A Personal Anthology

Compiled by

ALAN VILLIERS

ARCO PUBLISHING COMPANY, Inc.

NEW YORK

First published 1964 in the United States by
ARCO PUBLISHING COMPANY, INC.
NEW YORK N.Y.

Library of Congress Catalog Card Number: 64-12207
ARCO Catalog Number: 1178

Printed in Great Britain

CONTENTS

CONTENTS

The exacting life of the sea has this advantage over the life of the earth that its claims are simple and cannot be evaded

JOSEPH CONRAD: *Chance*

INTRODUCTION

THERE were sailing-ships at the bottom of our street—
real sailing-ships, I mean—Cape Horners, four-masted
barques, barques, full-rigged ships, and, now and again, a
big wooden skysail-yarder down from North America.
They lay in the berths of the Victoria Dock and along the
wharves in the Yarra, putting out clean yellow planks from
Scandinavia, great baulks of lumber from the Pacific
Slope, kerosene in cased square tins from New York, or,
when I was very young, general cargoes from Glasgow and
Liverpool and London. They towered over everything.
There were factory chimneys in the way, too, trying to
obscure the view, and the smell of the wool and hides
warehouses belonging to Messrs Dalgety or Goldsbrough
Mort was frequently an impediment to a fair view of anything.

I used to walk down and see these ships whenever I
could, with a favourite younger brother often, often alone.
Our father took us walks round the docks sometimes, too—
living geography, he called them, and he always pointed
out the various flags and cargoes. He was a man of modern
view and looked at the steamships too. We didn't. It was
the sailing-ships for us. Sometimes a steamship might be
interesting for a moment or so, an old-timer with thin
high stack, coming in with sails furled from running her
easting down on some long haul from the Cape of Good
Hope, or going out noisily from her berth in a haze of
blown-off steam and bad coal smoke and bellowings and
whistle-calls and yellings by dock pilots and such, and a
brace of tugs thrashing up the brown dock water, pulling
at them this way and that. But the sailing-ships were interesting always. They had only to stand quietly still at

9

their berths, and let the bay breezes orchestrate their maze of rigging. For me they were adventure, with a capital A!

I studied them from the age of seven, and kept notebooks about them.

As if all this were not enough, our father also read to us, when we were very young. He also liked the sea and its ships. Though an Australian born and bred, he and all that generation always had a feeling for the ships which had brought their fathers from Britain. Ships to him were not just ships, but a real link with so much of his faraway roots. To us children, they sufficed as ships, and when he read to us from Marryat, Clark Russell, Melville and the rest, the sea adventures sounded to us vivid and fascinating and real. We could connect them with the ships we knew and dream of adventures for ourselves in such vessels, in the dim and far-off future.

And indeed I dreamed. Those ships were links with Robinson Crusoe and the Swiss Family Robinson to me aged ten, and I went aboard them and climbed in the rigging, and talked with the sailors (usually of a Sunday morning, when they were sober and free) and dreamed not so much of just sailing with them. I would follow the life of fantastic adventure which seemed inexorably mixed up with them, a part of them, inevitable as the breaking sea and the blowing wind that gave them life.

I read for myself, too—in old books, mostly, because they were all I could afford. I bought books for a few pence from Coles Book Arcade, in the city, and at other emporiums which offered elderly tomes of all sorts by the thousand volumes.

I read new books from the library, too, always sea books. I read all the Marryats I could find, all the Clark Russells, all the Bullens (but there never was another to approach his *Cruise of the Cachalot*: I regretted that no *Cachalot*s nor any sort of whaling barque came then to Melbourne). I read and re-read Dana's *Two Years Before the Mast*, and found that wonderful. I discovered David Bone, and Conrad, and Masefield—seamen all, and wonderful writers. Bone's *Brassbounder* was my favourite childhood book for years, even ahead of Conrad's *Nigger of the Narcissus* and *Youth* and—yes, *Typhoon*, fascinating even though it was about a steamer.

Basil Lubbock's *Round the Horn Before the Mast* was factual stuff, dealing in detail with life aboard the ships I knew. I felt that Lubbock might turn up in the half-deck of any Limejuice Cape Horner at the Yarra wharves. And any brass-bound apprentice I saw coming down the gangplank of a Glasgow square-rigger, talking with his shipmates in a brogue to me then quite incomprehensible, might be a youthful Bone, any bearded mate or master of a trim Cape Horner could be the thoughtful Captain Conrad.

I felt instinctively that any ship he had to do with would be a well-kept and graceful vessel.

The years passed, slowly. No longer did the sailing liners come to Yarra wharves or to Port Melbourne. The graceful small iron sailing-ships, the thousand-ton *Lochs* and two-thousand ton Scottish *Shires*, the gracious *Glens* and *Clans* were gone. Some returned under the Norwegian, Swedish, and Russian flags, but by the second decade of the century their places were taken by massive ships, wall-sided four-masted barques which could carry five thousand tons and spent weeks loading bagged grain in a very leisurely fashion at the Williamstown wharves. The pretty little three- and four-masted schooners down from the Pacific Slope became huge five-masters, enormous ships of wood which often arrived with their maindecks awash, so deeply were they laden with their lumber, and the schooner crews were incredibly small. As they towed up-river I could count them—three men up for'ard to tend the lines with the mate, a couple aft with the second, one at the wheel, one tending the donkey-boiler—that was the crew. One man a mast! And the masts cut from the loftiest and most enormous pines the world had ever grown, the sails tremendous pieces of white cotton canvas, stiff and intractable.

I could find no books about these. Bullen, Russell, Lubbock, Bone, Melville, Dana, Conrad, and all the rest, apparently, had kept out of these Pacific ships. Some Yankee ships I noticed (not so much those from the West Coast but the Down Easters, those from the eastern seaboard of America) came into port in beautiful condition, like yachts—masts and yards perfectly varnished, spotless decks white and smooth and flawless no matter what gross bulk cargo they might have aboard, canvas all stowed with smooth perfection, the whole ship so perfect it looked as if a hundred men had done nothing for months but keep her clean and polish, scrub and furbish her appointments with loving care.

Aboard the skys'l yard barque *Montauk* I counted a crew of twenty-four, and I saw her go out with some of them chained to her bulwarks, and read in the newspaper *Age* how her mate—some big tough fellow from Nova Scotia—had bitten off a sailor's ear in a slight altercation while the barque sailed up Port Philip Bay.

Perhaps there was good reason for not going in these Yankee vessels.

According to my father, there was good reason for not going in *any* vessels, sail or steam, under any flag whatever. A dog's life, he said: but I had not gathered that from the books, not even from Dana.

So my father drew my attention to Dr Johnson's remarks upon the wretchedness of the sea life, as recorded by the industrious Boswell:

I again visited him on Monday. He took occasion to enlarge, as he often did, upon the wretchedness of a sea-life. "A ship is worse than a gaol. There is, in a gaol, better air, better company, better conveniency of every kind; and a ship has the additional disadvantage of being in danger. When men come to like a sea-life, they are not fit to live on land."—"Then" (said I) "it would be cruel in a father to breed his son to the sea." JOHNSON: "It would be cruel in a father who thinks as I do. Men go to sea, before they know the unhappiness of that way of life; and when they have come to know it, they cannot escape from it, because it is then too late to choose another profession; as indeed is generally the case with men, when they have once engaged in any particular way of life."

JAMES BOSWELL: *The Life of Samuel Johnson*

This was all very well, this pontificating stuff with its air

12

of authority. But who was this Dr Johnson? Had he ever been at sea? He had produced a wonderful dictionary, I was told. So I had a look at this dictionary. It was obvious at a glance, even with just the background of ship knowledge that I had then acquired, that the pompous doctor knew nothing about ships at all, whatever else he might have known. His definitions of the simplest shipboard terms were so inaccurate as to be stupid.

"*Topsail,* the highest sail," I read, and for *Topgallant* precisely the same definition. How could they both be the highest sail? Topgallant is not the name of a sail anyway but of a mast: topgallant-*sail* is the name of the sail and, even in the loquacious doctor's day there had been another sail above it—the royal—for at least a century. I read on under "T". "*Tiller,* the rudder of a boat." Tiller a *rudder*? What was the old ass talking about? Any sea scout on Albert Park Lake could do better than he was doing! His guesses for "S" were no better. *Shrouds,* I saw, were for him "the sail-ropes. It seems to be taken sometimes for the sails". What! Hadn't he ever talked with a sailor? Shrouds are part of the standing rigging.

To belay, to luff, to overhaul—he understands none of the terms but lays down an erroneous definition for them all. To belay, to him, is "to splice, to mend a rope by laying one end over another". Is it, indeed? I had seen the rows of belaying pins aboard every square-rigger that docked in Melbourne, with their gear carefully "belayed" round them, each piece of essential cordage for working the sails or swinging the yards aollcated its own pin and properly belayed around it. A belaying pin holds a rope fast, which has been secured to it.

Hadn't Dr Johnson ever heard during his peregrinations in the great seaport of London the shout ashore to "Belay there! Belay!" meaning to make an end, to be done with something, to secure it? For the illustrious doctor, too, to "overhale"—the word then current for our "overhaul"—is "to spread over"; to "luff" is to "go to a distance". Luff then was "loof" but it meant then just what it still means, to come up to the wind.

"Luff her up there, luff her up!" Captain Suffern shouted

13

at us boys sailing his brigantine-rigged old lifeboat on the Albert Park Lake whenever a squall struck us. If we had "gone to a distance" on that order, it had better be a pretty long distance!

There were excuses for the Johnson errors. The sea lingo is not for everyone. As that indefatigable producer of Naval Tracts, the Elizabethan Sir William Monson, points out, "The sea language is not soon learned and much less understood, being only proper to him that has served his apprenticeship: besides that a boisterous sea and stormy weather will make a man not bred to it so sick that it bereaves him of legs, stomach, and courage so much as to fight with his meat. . . ."

I thought that Dr Johnson must have produced some of his dictionary in a boisterous sea indeed. As for his views on the wretchedness of the sea life, the opinionated, pigheaded old ass was welcome to them. They had no effect on me.

About this time, when I was perhaps thirteen (and was trying for entry to Australia's Naval College at Jervis Bay under the impression that I might relive some Marryat adventures in that service: the Australian Naval Board, very fortunately, would have none of me) I began to wonder about some of the writers whose work I'd been studying so carefully. This Clark Russell, for instance—he certainly wrote some yarns which I enjoyed when young, though I preferred Frank Bullen. I began to wonder how pigheaded he might be, too, when I read some of his later stuff and compared what he said with what I could see for myself.

"It is impossible to admire the typical iron sailing-ship," I read with astonishment in Clark Russell's *The Ship, Her Story* of 1899, when iron ships, surely, had been doing good work for half a century.

"Nothing that is beautiful with wings is left to us but the yacht." Good heavens! Hadn't the lugubrious pundit ever seen or heard of a South Seas brigantine, a Tasman Sea schooner, or beheld *any* of those magnificent iron beauties such as the *Coriolanus*, the *Mermerus*, Conrad's little barque

Otago and all the multitude of their gracious, able, and sweet-lined kind? Didn't he think there could be a perfect metal ship *at all*?

Apparently he did not. He *had* seen them or some of them.

"The iron sailing-ship need not thrust herself in," he pontifies. "They show you the *France*—she was, a little while ago, the biggest sailing-ship in the world [1894]: they may have launched a huger since—they expect admiration whilst you gaze; you cannot admire, you can but mourn. She is ugly enough with her forest of spars when everything is furled, and all her gear is hauled tight and the yards squared by lift and brace—which is a rare manœuvre aboard a merchantman in this age: but then they have sheeted home and manned the halliards—my precious eyes!—clews a fathom from the yardarms; here a topgallant-sail arching into sheer monstrosity through cruel deprivation of quite necessary midship cloths; there a topsail hanging like an ill-fitting coat upon a man; yonder a flying-jib that, being set by mistake, should have the captain's initials in the corner: elsewhere all is blue sky or driving gloom beheld through labour-saving interstices."

One day I looked up on the river and towing in with the two-funnelled tug *James Patterson* proudly before her and the *Racer* astern came this magnificent and maligned steel five-masted barque *France*—huge indeed, with her steel masts double-yarded on all four topmasts and four topgallant-masts, her lower yards ninety feet long and her masts towering 160 feet above the graceful sheer of her long main deck. Aye, huge she was, but she was also nobly proportioned and beautifully sheered.

I had to count the masts twice to see she was a five-master, having seen schooners only with that many sticks before (some of them had six). I could see at a glance that there was a good deal of the unusual about her, but her oddness of rig was no blatant feature. In her own way and in my eyes, she looked just as *right* as any clipper did in hers.

Bigger ships were built, too—the greatest of them all the five-masted ship *Preussen* of Hamburg and her sister Laeisz liner *Potosi*, five-masted barque. These were in many ways the most magnificent and certainly the most powerful square-rigged ships ever built, and their performances stand unrivalled.

I wonder what Clark Russell might have thought of them! Not much, indeed: to some writers of his generation, it was sufficient that the *France* was French and the *Potosi* German to put them beyond the pale. They were writers, not sailors. Sailors have been international down the centuries. But perhaps they have been biased men, too, in that each generation has loved its own. The lover of the old wooden walls and the wood-built merchantmen at least could plead that he and his kind had had some centuries to get used to them, with little change.

When that five-masted *France* came up the Yarra, I knew I would go to the deep water under sail, and see for myself—aye, and maybe collect some bias of my own, though I hoped to be not quite so bigoted.

BEFORE GOING TO SEA

The Build-up

BEFORE GOING TO SEA

The Build-up

AT Sunday School in North Melbourne, we heard about the shipwreck of St Paul. I studied the story in the Acts of the Apostles but could not make much of it then. About all I could grasp was that the ship—a fair-sized one to carry all those people—must have been delayed so as to miss her ordinary sailing season and this was the fundamental reason for her troubles. But sailing season for ships? What could that be? The ships I knew made a sailing season of the year round. The Mediterranean was a long way from Melbourne, but I learned at school to regard it as a sea of good weather, particularly the eastern end whence St Paul sailed. (I learned a little better later—much later, during the Second World War.)

And anchors over the *stern*? (I had to wait until the Second World War to see them, too. The landing ships in my Combined Operations Squadron had them, but this was to haul themselves off beaches up which they ran bows first.)

I could appreciate, very early, that the ship's people probably did not care to listen to St Paul admonishing them, however right he might have been.

I had to sail with the Arabs in their big Indian Ocean dhows (vessels rather like St Paul's must have been, in many ways) before really appreciating the shipwreck story at its true worth, and comprehending what the seamen did. They "strake sail, and so were driven": they lowered their big sail and let her drive, under bare poles. They anchored by the stern because the hull was so shaped that it lay better in a strong wind that way, and their anchors were easily portable. They had big crews, for the gear was primitive, the work

19

heavy, and the seamen were also the stevedores. Nor was the ship necessarily very large to carry 276 persons. One Kuwait dhow I was to sail in later carried that number for a couple of months, and she was a two-master of 150 tons. (The people lived anywhere, camping on deck as they could. There was no accommodation as we know it, nor was it missed.)

The shipmen "loosed the rudder bands" to save the rudder from damage when the ship beached. I saw Arab dhows at Muscat with just such rudder-bands, which were loosed whenever the dhows lay in port, and the rudder hauled up out of harm's way. These were a particular kind of dhow called *bedeni*.

All these things I was to discover later. As a child, I read and wondered. How was it that St Paul knew about ships?

"Except these abide in the ship, ye cannot be saved," he remarked to the Centurion when the crew tried to go off in the longboat which they had got ready while pretending to clear the anchors.

The Centurion should not have needed to be told: but it was good advice.

The Shipwreck of St Paul

And when it was determined that we should sail into Italy, they delivered Paul and certain other prisoners unto one named Julius, a centurion of Augustus' band. And entering into a ship of Adramyttium, we launched, meaning to sail by the coasts of Asia, one Aristarchus, a Macedonian of Thessalonica, being with us.

And the next day we touched at Sidon, and Julius courteously entreated Paul, and gave him liberty to go unto his friends to refresh himself. And when we had launched from thence, we sailed under Cyprus, because the winds were contrary. And when we had sailed over the sea of Cilicia and Pamphylia, we came to Myra, a city of Lycia. And there the centurion found a ship of Alexandria sailing into Italy, and he put us therein.

And when we had sailed slowly many days, and scarce were come over against Cnidus, the wind not suffering us, we sailed under Crete, over against Salmone. And, hardly passing it, came unto a place which is called The Fair Havens, nigh whereunto was the city of Lasea.

Now when much time was spent, and when sailing was now dangerous, because the fast was now already past, Paul admonished them, and said unto them:

Sirs, I perceive that this voyage will be with hurt and much damage, not only of the lading and ship, but also of our lives.

Nevertheless the centurion believed the master and the owner of the ship more than those things which were spoken by Paul, and because the haven was not commodious to winter in, the more part advised to depart thence also, if by any means they might attain to Phenice, and there to winter, which is an haven of Crete and lieth toward the south west and north west. And when the south wind blew softly, supposing that they had obtained their purpose, loosing thence, they sailed close by Crete.

But not long after there arose against a tempestuous wind called Euroclydon; and when the ship was caught, and could not bear up into the wind, we let her drive. And running under a certain island which is called Clauda, we had much work to come by the boat, which when they had taken up, they used helps, undergirding the ship; and fearing lest they should fall into the quicksands, strake sail, and so were driven.

And we being exceedingly tossed with a tempest, the next day they lightened the ship. And the third day we cast out with our own hands the tackling of the ship; and when neither sun nor stars in many days appeared, and no small tempest lay on us, all hope that we should be saved was then taken away.

But after long abstinence, Paul stood forth in the midst of them, and said,

Sirs, ye should have hearkened unto me, and not have loosed from Crete, and to have gained this harm and loss; and now I exhort you to be of good cheer, for there shall be no loss of any man's life among you, but of the ship. For there stood by me this night the angel of God, whose I am, and whom I serve, saying, Fear not, Paul; thou must be brought before Caesar: and lo, God hath given thee all them that sail with thee. Wherefore, sirs, be of good cheer, for I believe God, that it shall be even as it was told me. Howbeit we must be cast upon a certain island.

But when the fourteenth night was come, as we were driven up and down in Adria, about midnight the shipmen deemed that they drew near to some country; and sounded and found it twenty fathoms. And when they had gone a little further, they sounded again, and found it fifteen fathoms. Then, fearing lest we should have fallen upon rocks, they cast four anchors out of the stern, and wished for the day.

And as the shipmen were about to flee out of the ship, when they had let down the boat into the sea, under colour as though they would have cast anchors out of the foreship, Paul said to the centurion and to the soldiers,

Except these abide in the ship, ye cannot be saved.

Then the soldiers cut off the ropes of the boat and let her fall off.

And while the day was coming on, Paul besought them all to take meat, saying,

This day is the fourteenth day that ye have tarried and continued fasting, having taken nothing. Wherefore I pray you to take some meat, for this is for your health; for there shall not an hair fall from the head of any of you.

And when he had thus spoken, he took bread and gave thanks to God in presence of them all, and when he had broken it he began to eat. Then were they all of good cheer, and they also took some meat. And we were in all in the ship two hundred threescore and sixteen souls. And when they had eaten enough, they lightened the ship, and cast out the wheat into the sea.

And when it was day, they knew not the land, but they discovered a certain creek with a shore, into the which they were minded, if it were possible, to thrust in the ship. And when they had taken up the anchors, they committed themselves unto the sea, and loosed the rudder bands, and hoisted up the mainsail to the wind, and made toward shore. And falling into a place where two seas met, they ran the ship aground, and the forepart stuck fast and remained unmoveable, but the hinder part was broken with the violence of the waves.

And the soldiers' counsel was to kill the prisoners lest any of them should swim out and escape. But the centurion, willing to save Paul, kept them from their purpose, and commanded that they which could swim should cast themselves first into the sea, and get to land, and the rest, some on boards, and some on broken pieces of the ship. And so it came to pass, that they escaped all safe to land.

From the ACTS OF THE APOSTLES, *Chapter* 27

WILLIAM SHAKESPEARE

At school we studied Shakespeare—plenty of good, gutsy stuff there! He knew about ships, too: or somebody did, and told him.

I liked especially the opening scene of *The Tempest*, though here again I had to wait until I had been at sea a long time before I fully understood what those sailors were doing. What was to "yare"? Why lower the topmast in a storm? Indeed, *how* could such a thing be done? "Bring her to try with main course." What sort of sea lingo was this?

In the iron ships Clark Russell scorned, I found the mariners knew as little as I. Nobody "yared" anything in them: the topmasts were of stoutest steel and could not be lowered (indeed, in several ships built during the 1890s, lowermasts and topmasts were combined in the one elongated steel cylinder): a main course we had, to be sure, but to bring the ship to try we never tried at all. Try what?

Shakespeare *might* have been at sea at some time during part of the eight unrecorded years of his life, from twenty to twenty-eight, between leaving Stratford and appearing in London. I doubt it. A gifted writer then as now could absorb technical detail to perfection, and quickly, if he put his mind to it. Look at Kipling (I liked his *Captains Courageous*, but his ultra-imperialist views did not go so well in Australia) and the Hornblower stories by C. S. Forester. A yarn with a sailing master, an observant morning aboard a bark in the Pool of London, and Shakespeare would have absorbed all he needed.

As for the seamanship of those days, I had to wait until I sailed the new *Mayflower* to America in 1957 before I knew about that. She was such a ship as Shakespeare might have studied. She had light topmasts which could be lowered in a gale, and light topsails that were taken in before the courses. She could be brought "a-try" with the main course, by half lowering the main yard, securing the sail's weather leech, slewing the weather end of the yard to the deck and letting the leeward end ride high so that only part of the sail was left set, like a lateen. In a very high wind, the *Tempest*'s mariners would have done that to keep some canvas on the ship, being near the land.

The Tempest

SCENE—*The Sea, with a Ship: afterwards an uninhabited Island.*

ACT I. SCENE I. *On a Ship at Sea—A Storm, with Thunder and Lightning.*

Enter a SHIPMASTER *and a* BOATSWAIN.

MASTER. Boatswain,—

BOATS. Here, master: what cheer?

MASTER. Good: Speak to the mariners: fall to't yarely, or we run ourselves aground, bestir, bestir.   [*Exit.*

Enter MARINERS.

BOATS. Heigh, my hearts; cheerly, cheerly, my hearts; yare, yare; take in the top-sail; 'Tend to the master's whistle.—Blow till thou burst thy wind, if room enough!

Enter ALONSO, SEBASTIAN, ANTONIO, FERDINAND, GONZALO *and others.*

ALON. Good Boatswain, have care. Where's the master? Play the men.

BOATS. I pray now, keep below.

ANT. Where is the master, Boatswain?

BOATS. Do you not hear him? You mar our labour;—keep your cabins: you do assist the storm.

GON. Nay, good, be patient.

BOATS. When the sea is. Hence! What care these roarers for the name of king? To cabin: silence and trouble us not.

GON. Good; yet remember whom thou hast aboard.

BOATS. None that I more love than myself. You are a counsellor: if you can command these elements to silence, and work the peace of the present, we will not hand a rope more; use your authority. If you cannot, give thanks you have lived so long, and make yourself ready in your cabin for the mischance of the hour, if it so hap.—Cheerly, good hearts.—Out of our way, I say.   [*Exit.*

GON. I have great comfort from this fellow: methinks he hath no drowning mark upon him; his complexion is perfect gallows. Stand fast, good fate, to his hanging! make the rope of his destiny our cable, for our own doth little advantage! If he be not born to be hanged, our case is miserable.   [*Exeunt.*

Re-enter BOATSWAIN.

BOATS. Down with the top-mast; yare; lower, lower; bring her to try with main-course. [*A cry within*] A plague upon this howling! They are louder than the weather, or our office.—

Re-enter SEBASTIAN, ANTONIO, *and* GONZALO.

Yet again? What do you here? Whall we give o'er and drown? Have you a mind to sink?

SEB. A pox o' your throat! you bawling, blasphemous, incharitable dog!

BOATS. Work you, then.

ANT. Hang, cur, hang! you whoreson, insolent noise-maker, we are less afraid to be drowned than thou art.

GON. I'll warrant him from drowning; though the ship were no stronger than a nutshell, and as leaky as an unstanchèd wench.

BOATS. Lay her a-hold, a-hold: set her two courses; off to sea again, lay her off.

Enter MARINERS, *wet.*

MAR. All lost! To prayers, to prayers! all lost!

[*Exeunt.*

BOATS. What, must our mouths be cold?

GON. The king and prince at prayers! let us assist them, For our case is as theirs.

SEB. I am out of patience.

ANT. We are merely cheated of our lives by drunkards.— This wide-chapp'd rascal:—Would thou mightst lie drowning, The washing of ten tides!

GON. He'll be hanged yet; Though every drop of water swear against it, And gape at wid'st to glut him.

[*A confused noise within,*—"Mercy on us!"—"We split, we split!"—"Farewell, my wife and children!"—"Farewell brother!" —"We split, we split, we split!"]

ANT. Let's all sink with the king. [*Exit.*

SEB. Let's take leave of him. [*Exit.*

GON. Now would I give a thousand furlongs of sea for an acre of barren ground; long heath, brown furze, any thing: The wills above be done! but I would fain die a dry death. [*Exeunt.*

DANA AND MELVILLE

Dana I liked, not only his *Two Years Before the Mast* but his Seaman's Manuals. Melville's *Moby Dick* was heavy going

25

for a boy. I preferred Bullen's red-blooded *Cachalot*. Richard Dana, scion of a well-known New England family, had become a lawyer by profession after going to sea in a brig out of Boston (1834–36) from Harvard University. He was an acute observer, and he could write.

I never did get through the whole of *Moby Dick*, without skipping: what stuck was astonishment at the appalling behaviour of the crazed Captain Ahab, and I hoped I would never find myself at sea with such as that peg-legged psychopath, nor in a whaler either. I need not have worried. The only whaler I was able to serve in was a 12,000-ton steamer, a pioneer floating factory of a thing called the *Sir James Clark Ross* which made the first pelagic whaling voyage into the Ross Sea in 1923–24. She was commanded by a great Norwegian named Carl Anton Larsen: her Ahabs were in a few of her five whale-catchers, independent commands, grim little ships in those icy, dangerous waters.

Dana I could thoroughly understand. I had the inestimable advantage of being able to walk down to the docks, and comprehend his seamanship, for a few such vessels were still about. The old brig *Edward* still came into the Little Dock, and I knew her Captain Shimmins. He would explain things to me.

I was lucky. It must be all Greek to lads today.

Doubling the Cape

With the wind about two points free, the yards braced in a little, and two close-reefed topsails and a reefed foresail on the ship, we made great way toward the southward; and almost every watch, when we came on deck, the air seemed to grow colder, and the sea to run higher. Still we saw no ice, and had great hopes of going clear of it altogether, when, one afternoon, about three o'clock, while we were taking a *siesta* during our watch below, "All hands!" was called in a loud and fearful voice. "Tumble up here, men!—tumble up!—don't stop for your clothes—before we're upon it!" We sprang out of our berths and hurried upon deck. The loud, sharp voice of the captain was heard giving orders, as though for life or death, and we ran aft to the braces, not waiting to look ahead, for not a moment was to be lost. The helm was hard up, the after yards shaking, and the ship in the act of wearing. Slowly, with the stiff ropes and iced rigging, we swung the yards round, everything coming hard and with a creaking and rending sound like pulling up a plank which has been frozen into the ice.

The ship wore round fairly, the yards were steadied, and we stood off on the other tack, leaving behind us, directly under our larboard quarter, a large ice island, peering out of the mist, and reaching high above our tops; while astern, and on either side of the island, large tracts of field-ice were dimly seen, heaving and rolling in the sea. We were now safe, and standing to the northward; but, in a few minutes more, had it not been for the sharp lookout of the watch, we should have been fairly upon the ice, and left our ship's old bones adrift in the Southern Ocean.

With a fair wind we soon ran clear of the field-ice, and by noon had only the stray islands floating far and near upon the ocean. The sun was out bright, the sea of a deep blue, fringed with the white foam of the waves, which ran high before a strong south-wester; our solitary ship tore on through the open water as though glad to be out of her confinement; and the ice islands lay scattered here and there, of various sizes and shapes, reflecting the bright rays of the sun, and drifting slowly northward before the gale. It was a contrast to much that we had lately seen, and a spectacle not only of beauty, but of life; for it required but little fancy to imagine these islands to be animate masses which had broken loose from the "thrilling regions of thick-ribbed ice," and were working their way, by wind and current, some alone, and some in fleets, to milder climes. No pencil has ever yet given anything like the true effect of an iceberg. In a picture, they are huge, uncouth masses, stuck in the sea, while their chief beauty and grandeur—their slow, stately motion, the whirling of the snow about their summits, and the fearful groaning and cracking of their parts—the picture cannot give. This is the large iceberg, —while the small and distant islands, floating on the smooth sea, in the light of a clear day, look like little floating fairy isles of sapphire.

From a northeast course we gradually hauled to the eastward, and after sailing about two hundred miles, which brought us as near to the western coast of Terra del Fuego as was safe, and having lost sight of the ice altogether,—for the third time, we put the ship's head to the southward, to try the passage of the Cape.

Having a fine wind, we were soon up with and passed the latitude of the Cape, and having stood far enough to the southward to give it a wide berth, we began to stand to the eastward, with a good prospect of being round and steering to the northward on the other side in a very few days. But ill luck seemed to have lighted upon us. Not four hours had we been standing on in this course before it fell dead calm, and in half an hour it clouded up, a few straggling blasts, with spits of snow and sleet, came from the eastward, and in an hour more we lay hove-to under a close-reefed main topsail, drifting bodily off to leeward before the fiercest storm that we had yet felt, blowing dead ahead, from the eastward. It seemed as though the genius of the place had been roused at finding that we had nearly slipped through his fingers, and had come down upon us with tenfold fury. The sailors said that every blast, as it shook the shrouds, and whistled through the rigging, said to the old ship, "No, you don't!"—"No, you don't!"

For eight days we lay drifting about in this manner. Sometimes—generally towards noon—it fell calm; once or twice a round copper ball showed itself for a few moments in the place where the sun ought to have been, and a puff or two came from the westward, giving some hope that a fair wind had come at last. During the first two days we made sail for these puffs, shaking the reefs out of the topsails and boarding the tacks of the courses; but finding that it only made work for us when the gale set in again, it was soon given up, and we lay-to under our close-reefs. We had less snow and hail than when we were farther to the westward, but we had an abundance of what is worse to a sailor in cold weather—drenching rain.

Our watches below were no more varied than the watch on deck. All washing, sewing, and reading was given up, and we did nothing but eat, sleep, and stand our watch, leading what might be called a Cape Horn life. The forecastle was too uncomfortable to sit up in; and whenever we were below, we were in our berths. To prevent the rain and the sea-water which broke over the bows from washing down, we were obliged to keep the scuttle closed, so that the forecastle was nearly air-tight. In this little, wet, leaky hole, we were all quartered, in an atmosphere so bad that our lamp, which swung in the middle from the beams, sometimes actually burned blue, with a large circle of foul air about it. Still, I was never in better health than after three weeks of this life. I gained a great deal of flesh, and we all ate like horses. At every watch when we came below, before turning in, the bread barge and beef kid were overhauled. Each man drank his quart of hot tea night and morning, and glad enough we were to get it; for no nectar and ambrosia were sweeter to the lazy immortals than was a pot of hot tea, a hard biscuit, and a slice of cold salt beef to us after a watch on deck. To be sure, we were mere animals, and, had this life lasted a year instead of a month, we should have been little better than the ropes in the ship.

RICHARD HENRY DANA: *Two Years Before the Mast*

They got round the Horn, of course, or Dana would never have written his book. I had no intention, at the age of twelve or so, of turning into any more of an animal than I then was. But we lads in Melbourne knew that Cape Horn was tough.

It wasn't so very far from us; all the homeward-bound sailing-ships in port had to go that way. Every one of those big square-riggers was a Cape Horner.

DANA ON THE SEAMAN'S LIFE

Two Years Before the Mast became the classic of that phase of the American seafaring life, and Dana's part in that hard voyage was about all I knew of him. Then one day in the Victoria Market at North Melbourne, browsing in a huge old clothes basket full of elderly books while my mother bargained with Chinese market gardeners for large supplies of fine fresh vegetables, I came across a little book in bright blue covers, with an anchor and a crown on the front cover.

"Dana's Seaman's Manual", the back binding said: the title page was full of descriptive stuff, as Victorian books used to be. It emerged at once that this was the authentic work of the Bostonian seaman-lawyer (but not sea-lawyer, which is a very different thing): what I had was the thirteenth edition, published in 1873, and this particular copy had somehow come to Melbourne from a bookshop in Yokohama. I bought it for threepence and I have it now. It was full of useful information, a good deal of it more or less legal—the protection of seamen from imposition, seamen's rights and duties, ship's business, and so forth.

The book, old as it was, certainly gave me a clear idea of what the seafaring profession was all about. Here, for instance, is Dana on ship masters, hitherto, to me at any rate, a mysterious and exalted breed:

The Master

The master has the entire control of the discipline of the ship, and no subordinate officer has authority to punish a seaman, or to use force, without the master's order, except in cases of necessity not admitting of delay. He has also the complete direction of the internal arrangements and economy of the vessel; and upon his character, and upon the course of conduct he pursues, depend in a great measure the character of the ship, and the conduct of both officers and men. He has a power and an influence, both direct and indirect, which may be the means of much good or much evil. If he is profane, passionate, tyrannical, indecent, or intemperate, more or less of the same qualities will spread themselves or break out among officers and men; which, perhaps, would have been checked if not in some degree removed, had the head of the ship been a man of high personal character. He may make his ship almost anything he chooses, and may render the lives and duties of his officers and men pleasant and profitable to them, or may introduce disagreements, discontent, tyranny, resistance, and, in fact, make the situation of all on board as uncomfortable as that in which any human beings can well be placed.

Also in the Seaman's Manual (always called the Seaman's Friend in the U.S.A.) is the following interesting résumé of what were then considered the duties of men rated as able seamen. The able seaman was a respected craftsman.

Able Seamen

Seafaring persons before the mast are divided into three classes —able seamen, ordinary seamen, and boys or green hands. And

30

it may be remarked here that all green hands in the merchant service are termed *boys,* and rated as such, whatever may be their age or size.

The crews are not rated by the officers after they get to sea, but, both in the merchant service and in the navy, each man rates himself when he ships. The shipping articles, in the merchant service, are prepared for so many of each class, and a man puts his name down and contracts for the wages and duty of a seaman, ordinary seaman, or boy, at his pleasure. Notwithstanding this license, there are very few instances of its being abused; for every man knows that if he is found incompetent to perform the duty he contracts for, his wages can not only be reduced to the grade for which he is fitted, but that something additional will be deducted for the deception practised upon all concerned, and for the loss of service and the numerous difficulties incurred, in case the fraud is not discovered until the vessel has got to sea. But still, more than this, the rest of the crew consider it a fraud upon themselves; as they are thus deprived of a man of the class the vessel required, which makes her short-handed for the voyage, and increases the duty put upon themselves. . . . Indeed, there is nothing a man can be guilty of, short of a felony, to which so little mercy is shown on board ship; for it is a deliberate act of deception.

The common saying that to hand, reef, and steer, makes a sailor, is a mistake. It is true that no man is a sailor until he can do these things; yet to ship for an able seaman he must, in addition to these, be a good workman upon rigging. The rigging of a ship requires constant mending, covering, and working upon a multitude of ways. . . . There is also a great deal of new rigging to be cut and fitted on board, which requires neat knots, splices, seizings, coverings, and turnings in. It is also frequently necessary to set up the rigging in one part of the vessel or another, in which case it must be seized or turned in afresh. . . . A man's skill in this work is the chief test of his seamanship; a competent knowledge of steering, reefing, furling, and the like, being taken for granted, and being no more than is expected of an ordinary seaman. To put a marlingspike in a man's hand, and set him to work upon a piece of rigging, is considered a fair trial of his qualities as an able seaman. . . . A seaman is generally expected to be able to sew upon a sail, and few men ship for seamen who cannot do it. . . .

No man is entitled to the rate or wages of an able seaman who is not a good helmsman. There is always a difference in a ship's company as to this duty, some men being more steady, careful, and expert helmsmen than others; and the best quality cannot be required of every able seaman; yet, if, upon fair trial, in bad weather, a seaman is found incapable of steering the ship, under circumstances not extraordinary, he would be considered by all on board to have failed of his duty. It should be remembered, however, that there are times when the very best helmsman is hardly able to steer a ship, and if a vessel is out of trim or slow in her motions, no skill can keep close to her course.

An able seaman is also expected to do all the work necessary for reefing, furling, and setting sail, to be able to take a bunt or bearing, to send yards or masts up and down, to rig in and out booms, to know how to reeve all the running rigging of a ship, and to steer, or pull an oar in a boat.

By the time I managed to get to sea in 1919, it appeared to me that there had been considerable deterioration in the excellent standards laid down by Bostonian Dana. His able seaman was of the days of *sail*: the powered ships' life was altogether different, and not a quarter as satisfying.

Dana's sailing-ship men had come down the centuries with very little change. An anonymous seventeenth-century poet gives a good picture of a seaman of his day which is, in its own way, very close to Dana's. I saw many seamen such as these coming ashore from sailing-ships in the Victoria Docks in Melbourne, and sailed with some in my first three ships.

The Seaman

He was a fellow brown of hue,
Sunburnt in his face he grew,
Well-set, strong of limb and bone,
Yet tight and yare as anyone.
Skill he had, the helm to steer,
And o' the ship's deck to domineer;
Each tackling, little rope, and line
He could find, when was no shine
Of sun or moon; in stormiest night
He could trim his sails aright.
His compass conned he at his heart,
And knew which winds blew in each part:
The stars he had as true by name

As if at font he heard the same;
And with his finger's point could tell
In what house every star did dwell
As here the Great Bear, that the Small,
Such stars are fixed, such shoot and fall
(At least they seemen down to slide),
There does the bright Orion glide,
The tailor's yard, and the stars seven
Is he acquainted with in heaven,
As well as those Seven Stars (the sign
To tell within is sold good wine).
Shelves, rocks, gulfs, quicksands, could he shun,
And in the main ocean his course run
By his good needle and his chard,
Blow grumbling Boreas ne'er so hard.

ANON. *17th century*

Of Chaucer's shipman, too, there was still more than a
trace, though I saw none "in a gown of falding to the knee".
They used oilskins in my day.

The Shipman

A shipman was there, hailing from the west:
For aught I know he was from Dartëmouth.
He rode upon a rouncy, as he couth,
In a gown of falding to the knee.
A dagger hanging on a lace had he
About his neck under his arm adown.
The hot summer had made his hew all brown;
And, certainly, he was a good fellow.
Full many a draught of wine had he withdrawn
From Bordeaux-ward, while that the chapman slept.
Of nice conscience took he no keep.
If that he fought, and had the upper hand,
By water he sent them home to every land.
But of his craft to reckon well his tides,
His streams and his dangers him besides,
His harbour and his moon, his pilotage,
There was none such from Hull to Carthage.
Hardy he was, and wise to undertake;
With many a tempest had his beard been shake.

33

He knew well all the havens, as they were,
From Gotland to the cape of Finistere,
And every creek in Brittany and in Spain;
His barge y-clepèd was the *Maudelayne*.

GEOFFREY CHAUCER

Herman Melville, that metaphysical seer of the seaman's life, put the case for the old-time sailor rather clearly, for him. Here are some remarks from his parable *Billy Budd*:

And the old-fashioned sailor, the veritable man-before-the-mast, the sailor from boyhood up, he, tho' indeed of the same species as a landsman, is in some respects singularly distinct from him. The sailor is frankness, the landsman is finesse. Life is not a game with the sailor, demanding the long head; no intricate game of chess where few moves are made in straightforwardness, and ends are attained by indirection; an oblique, tedious, barren game hardly worth that poor candle burnt out in playing it.

Yet, as a class, sailors are in character a juvenile race. Even their deviations are marked by juvenility. And this more especially holding true with the sailors of Billy's time. Then, too, certain things which apply to all sailors, do more pointedly operate here and there, upon the junior one. Every sailor, too, is accustomed to obey orders without debating them; his life afloat is externally ruled for him; he is not brought into that promiscuous commerce with mankind where unobstructed free agency on equal terms—equal superficially, at least—soon teaches one that unless upon occasion he exercise a distrust keen in proportion to the fairness of the appearance, some foul turn may be served him. A ruled undemonstrative distrustfulness is so habitual, not with businessmen so much, as with men who know their kind in less shallow relations than business, namely, certain men-of-the-world, that they come at last to employ it all but unconsciously; and some of them would very likely feel real surprise at being charged with it as one of their general characteristics.

THE POETRY OF THE SEA

All this Dana stuff was very well as an antidote to *Peter the Whaler* and all that. But it was very factual, and hardly inspiring. I suppose that, if the ships hadn't been so close to the end of our street, I'd not have taken much interest in it.

But there was also poetry. Our father read a lot of that to us (and wrote a good deal too, though not about the sea: he mostly wrote Australian sonnets for the Sydney *Bulletin*) and we were required to work through Palgrave's *Golden Treasury*, among other works, in our English classes at Essendon High School. This was no work to me.

Shelley, for instance—Percy Bysshe Shelley. He could get through even my thick head, at least with much of his poetry. As for the sea, he was drowned in it, and this was a fate liberally forecast for myself whenever I mentioned my ambition to go off in deep-sea sail.

It was the *sea*, not ships, which moved Shelley. It was ships that moved me. But anyone who had sailed about Melbourne's Rip in bad weather, or looked upon the breakers round Barwon Heads, knew what he was saying in his "Unfathomable Sea!".

Unfathomable Sea!

Unfathomable Sea! whose waves are years!
   Ocean of Time, whose waters of deep woe
Are brackish with the salt of human tears!
   Thou shoreless flood which in thy ebb and flow
Claspest the limits of mortality,
And, sick of prey, yet howling on for more,
Vomitest thy wrecks on its inhospitable shore!
Treacherous in calm, and terrible in storm,
   Who shall put forth on thee,
      Unfathomable Sea?

PERCY BYSSHE SHELLEY

John Masefield wrote of the sailor's sea, the sea of sailing-ships. Later on, steamship men were inclined to belittle his "Sea Fever". Sailing-ship men didn't.

Sea Fever

I must down to the seas again, to the lonely sea and the sky,
And all I ask is a tall ship and a star to steer her by,
And the wheel's kick and the wind's song and the white sail's
    shaking,
And a grey mist on the sea's face and a grey dawn breaking.

I must down to the seas again, for the call of the running tide
Is a wild call and a clear call that may not be denied;
And all I ask is a windy day with the white clouds flying,
And the flung spray and the blown spume, and the sea-gulls
    crying.

I must down to the seas again, to the vagrant gypsy life,
To the gull's way and the whale's way where the wind's like a
    whetted knife;
And all I ask is a merry yarn from a laughing fellow-rover,
And quiet sleep and a sweet dream when the long trick's over.

From our class studies of poetry at school, I remembered
many things. I would read them and re-read them, and
dream of ships, which was not what the English master
sought at all.

On the Loss of the "Royal George"

Toll for the brave—
The brave that are no more:
    All sunk beneath the wave,
Fast by their native shore.
    Eight hundred of the brave,
Whose courage well was tried,
    Had made the vessel heel
And laid her on her side;
    A land-breeze shook the shrouds,
And she was overset;
    Down went the Royal George,
With all her crew complete.

WILLIAM COWPER

36

Home Thoughts, from the Sea

Nobly, nobly Cape Saint Vincent to the north-west died away;
Sunset ran, one glorious blood-red, reeking into Cadiz Bay;
Bluish 'mid the burning water, full in face Trafalgar lay;
In the dimmest north-east distance dawned Gibraltar grand and
    gray;
"Here and here did England help me: how can I help England?"
    —say,
Whoso turns as I, this evening, turn to God to praise and pray,
While Jove's planet rises yonder, silent over Africa.

ROBERT BROWNING

A Passer-By

Whither, O splendid ship, thy white sails crowding,
Leaning across the bosom of the urgent west,
That fearest nor sea rising nor sky clouding,
Whither away, fair rover, and what thy quest?

ROBERT BRIDGES

Where Lies the Land to Which the Ship Would Go?

Where lies the land to which the ship would go?
Far, far ahead, is all her seamen know.
And where the land she travels from? Away,
Far, far behind, is all that they can say.

On sunny noons upon the deck's smooth face,
Linked arm in arm, how pleasant here to pace;
Or, o'er the stern reclining, watch below
The foaming wake far widening as we go,

On stormy nights when wild north-westers rave,
How proud a thing to fight with wind and wave!
The dripping sailor on the reeling mast
Exults to bear, and scorns to wish it past.

Where lies the land to which the ship would go?
Far, far ahead, is all her seamen know.
And where the land she travels from? Away,
Far, far behind, is all that they can say.

ARTHUR HUGH CLOUGH

Port After Stormy Seas

What if some little pain the passage have,
That makes frail flesh to fear the bitter wave?
Is not short pain well borne that brings long ease,
And lays the soul to sleep in quiet grave?
Sleep after toil, port after stormy seas,
Ease after war, death after life does greatly please.

EDMUND SPENSER

Drake's Drum

Drake he's in his hammock an' a thousand mile away,
  (Capten, art tha sleepin' there below?)
Slung atween the round shot in Nombre Dios Bay,
  An' dreamin' arl the time o' Plymouth Hoe.
Yarnder lumes the Island, yarnder lie the ships,
  Wi' sailor-lads a-dancin' heel-an'-toe,
An' the shore lights flashin', an' the night-tide dashin',
  He sees et arl so plainly as he saw et long ago.

Drake he was a Devon man, an' ruled the Devon seas,
  (Capten, art tha sleepin' there below?)
Rovin' tho' his death fell, he went wi' heart at ease,
  An' dreamin' arl the time o' Plymouth Hoe.
"Take my drum to England, hang et by the shore,
  Strike et when your powder's runnin' low;
If the Dons sight Devon, I'll quit the port o' Heaven,
  An' drum them up the Channel as we drummed them long
    ago."

Drake he's in his hammock till the great Armadas come,
  (Capten, art tha sleepin' there below?)
Slung atween the round shot, listenin' for the drum,
  An' dreamin' arl the time o' Plymouth Hoe.
Call him on the deep sea, call him up the Sound,
  Call him when ye sail to meet the foe;
Where the old trade's plyin' an' the old flag flyin'
  They shall find him ware an' wakin', as they found him long
    ago!

SIR HENRY NEWBOLT

I read all the stories of voyages and exploration that I could find—of the early Portuguese, who came about the Australian coasts to the north and north-west long, long before the famed Captain Cook came to the east; of Drake and Anson and Dampier and all those; of Byron and Carteret and Bougainville in the South Seas; of D'Entrecasteaux, Matthew Flinders, and the mysterious La Perouse.

All these were fascinating and their stories were inspiring. The way in which those Portuguese pioneers groped down the dark coast of all West Africa towards the Cape of Good Hope and at last swept with their European ships into the Indian Ocean (at our back door) and made the discovery of Australia in due course inevitable—here was a moving sea affair to think about.

I found some battered old Hakluyt Society publications in that Melbourne market, and I treasured them. I was to sail with the Portuguese later, a good deal, and to admire them greatly. European princes of any sort were far removed from us, but the idea of the Portuguese (and half-English) Prince Henry sending off his pilots and his courtiers and adventurous seamen, from his own country and from Italy, always fascinated me. Why did they take so long to do what to us appeared so simple, to find a way from Portugal to the Indian Ocean? Only slowly did the reality of the tremendous difficulties overcome by those pioneers, and the immensity of the task their Prince undertook, dawn on me. That it ever did was no thanks to the history learned at school.

I remember the shock of discovering that history was no dull business of dates and events, of precise learning of well-established facts. The "facts" were in question. Our school-books did not mention the Portuguese in any Australian connection. They began and ended with James Cook, and there was a very great deal they left out about almost everything. I began to suspect there was even more which they presented—well, with bias.

But there was a Hakluyt Society, in London, which specialised in making good something of the more usual historical deficiencies, especially in matters concerned with voyages and discoveries, which meant (to me) ships and the sea.

In a Hakluyt Society book I read, for instance, about the quiet bravery of long-dead Portuguese, on some of these early African voyages—not legendary figures from a long-dead past, but real people, going about dangerous voyages with bravery and immense endurance.

Like, for example, Nuno Tristram.

How the Page of Prince Henry the Navigator Brought Home the Ship*

Ah, in what brief words did I find enregistered the record of the death of such a noble Knight as was this Nuno Tristram, of whose sudden end I purpose to speak. And of a surety I could not pass it by without tears, did I not know, almost by divine forecast, the eternal delight his soul tasteth, for it seemeth to me that I should be reckoned an covetous by all true Catholics were I to bewail the death of one whom it hath pleased God to make a sharer in His immortality. . . .

Now this noble knight was perfectly informed of the great desire and purpose of our virtuous Prince, being one who from such an early youth had been brought up in his household; and seeing how the Prince was toiling to send his ships to the land of the Negroes and much further yet, if he might accomplish it; and hearing that some caravels had already passed the river of Nile, and the things that were reported from there; it seemed to him that if he were not to make himself one of that elect company and to render service to the Infante his lord in that land in any good thing that might be done or encountered there, he could not obtain the name of a good man and true.

Wherefore he straightway made him ready a caravel, and having it armed, he began his voyage and stayed not in any part, but pursued his course toward the land of the Negroes. And passing by Cape Verde, he went sixty leagues further on and came unto a river, in which it seemed to him that there ought to be some inhabited places. Wherefore he caused to be launched two small boats he was carrying, and in them there entered twenty-two men, to wit, ten in one and twelve in the other. As they began to take their way up the river, the tide was rising with the which they

* Translated by the late Professor Edgar Prestage.

entered, and they made for some habitations that they espied on the right hand. And it came to pass that before they went on shore, there appeared from the other side twelve boats, in the which there would be as many as seventy or eighty Guineas, all Negroes, with bows in their hands. And because the water was rising, one of the boats of the Guineas crossed to the other side and put on shore those it was carrying, and thence they began to shoot arrows at our men in the boats. And the others who remained in the boats bestirred themselves as much as they could to get at our men, and as soon as they perceived themselves to be within reach, they discharged that accursed ammunition of theirs all full of poison upon the bodies of our countrymen. And so they held on in pursuit of them until they had reached the caravel which was lying outside the river in the open sea; and they were all hit by those poisoned arrows in such wise that before they came on board four of them died in the boats.

And so, wounded as they were, they made fast their small boats to the ship, and commenced to make ready for their voyage, seeing their case how perilous it was; but they were not able to lift their anchors for the multitude of arrows with which they were attacked, and they were constrained to cut the cables so that not one remained. And so they began to make sail, leaving the boats behind, for they could not hoist them up. And it came to pass that of the twenty-two men that left the ship only two escaped, to wit, one André Diaz and another Alvaro da Costa, both esquires of the Infante and natives of the City of Evora; and the remaining nineteen died, for that poison was so artfully composed that a slight wound, if it only let blood, brought men to their last end. And there died that noble Knight Nuno Tristram, very desirous as he was of this present life, in that there was no place left him to buy his death like a brave man. And there died also another Knight called John Correa, and one Duarte Dollanda, and Estevan Dalmeida, and Diego Machado, men of noble birth and young in years, brought up by the Infante in his household; as well as other esquires and foot-soldiers of the same upbringing; and seamen and others of the ship's company.

Suffice it to say that they numbered in all twenty-one, for of the seven that had remained in the caravel, two were also wounded as they were trying to raise the anchors. But whom will you have to make ready this ship that she may pursue her voyage, and depart from among that evil race? For the two esquires who remained, as we said, did not wholly escape from that peril, for being wounded they came near unto death, and lay ill quite twenty days, not being able to render any aid to the others who were toiling to direct the caravel. And these latter were not more than five in number, to wit, a sailor who was very little acquainted with the act of navigating, and a boy of the Infante's household called Airas Tinoco, who went as purser, and a Guinea boy who had been captured with the first prisoners taken in that land, and two other boys, both quite young, who were living with some of those esquires that died there. Of a surety, compassion is due to their great toil at that hour. They went weeping and sorrowing for the death of such a captain and of the others their comrades and friends, and were from that time in fear of the hateful enemies they knew to be near them, from whose deadly wounds so many and such brave men had died in a very brief space. And especially they sorrowed because they found so slight a remedy whereby to seek their safety; for the sailor lad in whom they were all putting their hope, confessed openly his scant knowledge, saying that he knew not how to direct the course of a ship or to work at anything of that kind in such wise as to be serviceable; but only if directed by another he would do what he could, as he was bidden.

O Thou great and supreme succour of all the forsaken and afflicted who dost never desert those that cry out to Thee in their most great necessity, and who now didst hear the cries of these men who made their moan to Thee, fixing their eyes on the height of the clouds and calling upon Thee to hasten to their aid; clearly didst Thou show that Thou heardest their prayers when in such a brief space Thou didst send them heavenly aid. For Thou didst give courage and understanding to a youth who had been born and brought up in Olivenca, an inland town far removed from the sea; and he, enlightened by divine grace, piloted the ship, and bade the seamen steer directly to the North, declining a little to the East, namely, to the wind that is called North-east, for he thought that there lay the kingdom of Portugal, towards which they wished to make their voyage. And as they were going thus on their way, after a part of the day was over, they went to see Nuno Tristram and the other wounded men, and they found them dead, so that they were obliged to throw them into the sea; and on that day they threw in fifteen, and four remained in the boats, and two they threw in the next day. But I write not of the feelings that would be theirs when they cast those bodies upon the multitude of waters, burying their flesh in the bellies of fish. For what importeth it to us if our bodies lack sepulture? since in our flesh we shall see our Saviour, according to the determination of Holy Scripture, for it is the same thing whether we lie in the sea or the land, and whether we be eaten of fishes or of birds. Our chief concern is in those works of ours by which after our death we shall find the truth of all these matters that here we see in figure. . . . Therefore we can say with justice to these men: "Beati mortui qui in Domino moriuntur." And moreover, all who read this history will obtain a reward from God, if they make a memorial of the death of these men in their prayers, for inasmuch as they died in the service of God and their lord, their death is happy.

Now this youth whom I have mentioned was that same Airas Tinoco of whom I spoke above, and in him God put such grace that for two months together he directed the course of that ship; but all were doubtful what their end would be, for in all those two months they never caught sight of land. And at the end of this time they sighted a pinnace which was on warlike business, and they had great fear at the sight, for they thought it belonged to Moors; but after they found it pertained to a Galician pirate whose name was Pero Falcom, a new joy came upon them, and much more so when they were told that they were off the coast of Portugal, opposite a place belonging to the Mastership of Santiago, called Sines. And so they arrived at Lagos, and thence they went to the Infante to tell him of the tragical fortune of their voyage, and laid before him a multitude of arrows by the which their companions had died.

GOMEZ EANNES DE ZURARA

SEA FICTION—CONRAD THE INIMITABLE

In the realm of sea fiction my tastes were catholic, but of course it was Conrad who really wrote most movingly and convincingly. Here was obviously a seaman who knew his subject with a knowledge that was both profound and intimate, and he could write profoundly of it too. I felt that, even before I went to sea. The convincing and stirring prose of the brooding Polish-English master mariner was the work of a master writer: ahead of him came nobody. After him there need come nobody, too, for in sail at least, he had said it all, convincingly, thoroughly, movingly, finally and for ever.

He had thought through to the essential truth and he had written it all, perfectly.

I never intended to write anything: I just appreciated and enjoyed Conrad. I was not going to sea to write! I meant to be Master of a Cape Horn ship—no more, no less. And Conrad made that calling very real.

After all, he had spent half a lifetime serving ships— ships I knew, like the full-rigger *Torrens,* and the barque *Otago.* These were vessels in the Australian trade. It was in the *Torrens* that he met John Galsworthy, aboard as passenger. It was the *Otago* which he sailed once on a memorable and most unusual passage through the Coral Sea and through Torres Straits, bound from Australia to Mauritius for a cargo of sugar.

Galsworthy describes him (in some lines written on Conrad's death in 1924):

It was in March, 1893, that I first met Conrad on board the English sailing ship *Torrens* in Adelaide Harbour. He was super-intending the stowage of cargo. Very dark he looked in the burning sunlight—tanned, with a peaked brown beard, almost black hair, and dark brown eyes, over which the lids were deeply folded. He was thin, not tall, his arms very long, his shoulders broad, his head set rather forward. He spoke to me with a strong foreign accent. He seemed to me strange on an English ship. For fifty-six days I sailed in his company.

The chief mate bears the main burden of a sailing ship. All the first night he was fighting a fire in the hold. None of us seventeen passengers knew of it till long after. It was he who had most truck with the tail of that hurricane off the Leeuwin, and later with another storm. He was a good seaman, watchful of the weather; quick in handling the ship; considerate with the apprentices—we had a long, unhappy Belgian youth among them, who took unhandily to the sea and dreaded going aloft; Conrad compassionately spared him all he could. With the crew he was popular; they were individuals to him, not a mere gang; and long after he would talk of this or that among them, especially of old Andy the sail-maker: "I likèd that old fellow, you know." With the young second mate, a cheerful, capable young seaman, very English, he was friendly; and respectful, if faintly ironic, with his whiskered, stout old English captain. I was supposed to be studying navigation for the Admiralty Bar, and every day would work out the ship's position with the captain. On one side of the saloon table we would sit and check our observations on this important matter with those of Conrad, who would sit on the other side of the table and look at us a little quizzically. For Conrad had commanded ships, and his subordinate position on the *Torrens* was only due to the fact that he was then still convalescent from the Congo experience which had nearly killed him.

His hero is not the sea, but man in conflict with that cruel and treacherous element. Ships he loved, but the sea—no. Not that he ever abused it, or talked of it with aversion; he accepted it as he accepted all the inscrutable remorselessness of Nature.

Aye, Galsworthy has written well. Consider the following, typical of Conrad's inimitable ability to capture a sea mood.

A marvellous stillness pervaded the world, and the stars, together with the serenity of their rays, seemed to shed upon the earth the assurance of everlasting security. The young moon recurved, and shining low in the west, was like a slender shaving thrown up from a bar of gold, and the Arabian Sea, smooth and cool to the eye like a sheet of ice, extended its perfect level to the perfect circle of a dark horizon. The propeller turned without a check, as though its beat had been part of the scheme of a safe universe; and on each side of the Patna two deep folds of water, permanent and sombre, on the unwrinkled shimmer, enclosed within their straight and diverging ridges a few white swirls of foam bursting in a low hiss, a few wavelets, a few ripples, a few undulations that, left behind, agitated the surface of the sea for an instant after the passage of the ship, subsided splashing gently, calmed down at last into the circular stillness of water and sky with the black speck of the moving hull remaining everlastingly in its centre.

Consider, too, the tremendous power of the sea picture presented by Conrad in his *Nigger of the "Narcissus"*, the story of a jute ship's voyage home from India.

Meantime the *Narcissus,* with square yards, ran out of the fair monsoon. She drifted slowly, swinging round and round the compass, through a few days of baffling light airs. Under the patter of short warm showers, grumbling men whirled the heavy yards from side to side; they caught hold of the soaked ropes with groans and sighs, while their officers, sulky and dripping with rain water, unceasingly ordered them about in wearied voices. During the short respites they looked with disgust into the smarting palms of their stiff hands, and asked one another bitterly: "Who would be a sailor if he could be a farmer?" All the tempers were spoilt, and no man cared what he said. One black night, when the watch, panting in the heat and half-drowned with the rain, had been through four mortal hours hunted from brace to brace, Belfast declared that he would "chuck the sea for ever and go in a steamer." This was excessive, no doubt. Captain Allistoun, with great self-control, would mutter sadly to Mr Baker: "It is not so bad—not so bad," when he had managed to shove, and dodge, and manœuvre his smart ship through sixty miles in twenty-four hours. From the door-step of the little cabin, Jimmy, chin in hand, watched our dis-tasteful labours with insolent and melancholy eyes. We spoke to him gently—and out of his sight exchanged sour smiles.

Then again, with a fair wind and under a clear sky, the ship went on piling up the South Latitude. She passed outside Mada-gascar and Mauritius without a glimpse of the land. Extra lashings were put on the spare spars. Hatches were looked to. The steward in his leisure moments and with a worried air tried to fit washboards to the cabin doors. Stout canvas was bent with care. Anxious eyes looked to the westward, towards the cape of storms. The ship began to dip into a southwest swell, and the softly luminous sky of low latitudes took on a harder sheen from day to day above our heads: it arched high above the ship vibrat-ing and pale, like an immense dome of steel, resonant with the deep voice of freshening gales. The sunshine gleamed cold on the white curls of black waves. Before the strong breath of westerly squalls the ship, with reduced sail, lay slowly over, obstinate and yielding. She drove to and fro in the unceasing endeavour to fight her way through the invisible violence of the winds: she pitched headlong into dark smooth hollows; she struggled upwards over the snowy ridges of great running seas; she rolled, restless, from side to side, like a thing in pain. Endur-ing and valiant, she answered to the call of men; and her slim spars, waving for ever in abrupt semicircles, seemed to beckon in vain for help towards the stormy sky.

They watched the weather and the ship as men on shore watch the momentous chances of fortune. Captain Allistoun never left the deck, as though he had been part of the ship's fittings. Now and then the steward, shivering, but always in shirt sleeves, would struggle towards him with some hot coffee, half of which the gale blew out of the cup before it reached the master's lips. He drank what was left gravely in one long gulp, while heavy sprays pattered loudly on his oilskin coat, the seas swishing broke about his high boots; and he never took his eyes off the ship. He kept his gaze riveted upon her as a loving man watches the unselfish toil of a delicate woman upon the slender thread of whose existence is hung the whole meaning and joy of the world. We all watched her. She was beautiful and had a weakness. We loved her no less for that. We admired her qualities aloud, we boasted of them to one another, as though they had been our own, and the consciousness of her only fault we kept buried in the silence of our profound affection. She was born in the thundering peal of hammers beating upon iron, in black eddies of smoke, under a grey sky, on the banks of the Clyde. The clamorous and sombre stream gives birth to things of beauty that float away into the sunshine of the world to be loved by men.

The *Narcissus* was one of that perfect brood. Less perfect than many perhaps, but she was ours, and, consequently, incomparable. We were proud of her. In Bombay, ignorant landlubbers alluded to her as that "pretty grey ship". Pretty! A scurvy meed of commendation! We knew she was the most magnificent sea boat ever launched. We tried to forget that, like many good sea boats, she was at times rather crank. She was exacting. She wanted care in loading and handling, and no one knew exactly how much care would be enough. Such are the imperfections of mere men! The ship knew, and sometimes would correct the presumptuous human ignorance by the wholesome discipline of fear. We had heard ominous stories about past voyages.

Captain Allistoun, looking more hard and thin-lipped than ever, hung on to full topsails and foresail, and would not notice that the ship, asked to do too much, appeared to lose heart altogether for the first time since we knew her. She refused to rise, and bored her way sullenly through the seas. Twice running, as though she had been blind or weary of life, she put her nose deliberately into a big wave and swept the decks from end to end.

As the boatswain observed with marked annoyance, while we were splashing about in a body to try and save a worthless wash-tub: "Every blooming thing in the ship is going overboard this afternoon." Venerable Singleton broke his habitual silence and said with a glance aloft: "The old man's in a temper with the weather, but it's no good bein' angry with the winds of heaven."

The ship tossed about, shaken furiously, like a toy in the hand of a lunatic. Just at sunset there was a rush to shorten sail before the menace of a sombre hail cloud. The hard gust of wind came brutal like the blow of a fist. The ship, relieved of her canvas in time, received it pluckily; she yielded reluctantly to the violent onset; then, coming up with a stately and irresistible motion, brought her spars to windward in the teeth of the screeching squall. Out of the abysmal darkness of the black cloud overhead white hail streamed on her, rattled on the rigging, leaped in handfuls off the yards, rebounded on the deck—round and gleaming in the murky turmoil like a shower of pearls. It passed away. For a moment a livid sun shot horizontally the last rays of sinister light between the hills of steep, rolling waves. Then a wild night rushed in—stamped out in a great howl that dismal remnant of a stormy day.

There was no sleep on board that night. Most seamen remember in their life one or two such nights of a culminating gale. Nothing seems left of the whole universe but darkness, clamour, fury—and the ship. And like the last vestige of a shattered creation she drifts, bearing an anguished remnant of sinful mankind, through the distress, tumult and pain of an avenging terror.

JOSEPH CONRAD: The Nigger of the "Narcissus"

STORIES OF THE FABULOUS SOUTH SEAS

The port of Melbourne had not the same direct access to the South Seas as Sydney, but we were just as interested in the Pacific story. The copra barquentines (full of bugs) and schooners used Sydney as their home port, and the so-called "recruiting" schooners went to Queensland ports. These were slavers, really—blackbirders. A "blackbird" was any unfortunate Melanesian or Micronesian who survived a brutal kidnapping from his native islands and transport in a small foul hold to a sugar port in Queensland. Here he was landed as "contracted labour".

This traffic was pretty well regulated by the time I took an interest in ships, but I can remember an adventurous pair of uncles (gold prospectors in New Guinea) talking of the notorious blackbirder Bully Hayes as a person, not a myth, and a thoroughly despicable person at that. Bully had been a prominent pirate, ship-thief, and blackbirder, apparently. A shipmate had recently brained him at sea, and this my uncles viewed as a belated though very welcome removal from an otherwise more or less pleasant scene.

I never saw Bully Hayes (he came from Cleveland, Ohio, of all places: and he'd stolen ships all round Australia and New Zealand). Lawful sea warfare was one thing— Marryat's stuff, and Lord Cochrane stealing the frigate *Esmeralda* from the very batteries of Callao, the Japanese beating up the incredible Russian fleet at Tsushima, and so forth—but swine like the swashbuckling W. H. Hayes of Cleveland and the South Seas got better men killed. I never could see the "romance" of piracy—a dirty, treacherous calling. Through their appalling behaviour towards the peaceful (well, more or less) peoples of the S.W. Pacific Islands, pirates and blackbirders such as Hayes caused Commodore Goodenough to be murdered, and many an innocent trader or whaler to be cut out in some lovely lagoon, and all her people butchered.

There was plenty of real adventure in those South Seas, for all that. I was always interested, for instance, in the story of a colourful character named Roberton, or Robertson, who had been with Lord Cochrane in the fight for the liberation of Chile and Peru. This Roberton turned up in Australia later.

Thomas Dunbabin, once a Tasmanian Rhodes Scholar and later a newspaper editor in Sydney and London, gives something of his story in a book called *Slavers of the South Seas*.

William Smith, master of the schooner *Caledonia,* sailing out of Port Dalrymple in Van Diemen's Land, was well acquainted with the islands of Bass Straits and their motley inhabitants. He was a hardy and resourceful mariner who had in 1825 careened and repaired his schooner on the shores of Westernport, in the wilderness that was to be later the colony of Victoria. Lacking tar and pitch for his seams he contrived to make shift with a substitute, melting down the gum of the grass trees or Xanthorrheas which were abundant in that region. In 1826 the captain of the *Caledonia,* going about his business in the Straits, met amongst the sealers of Cape Barren Island a dark mysterious stranger with a Spanish look who suggested a voyage that might yield more profit, and perhaps more excitement, than the business of picking up cargoes of sealskins, wallaby skins, wattle bark and such things amongst the islands or along the southern coasts of Australia.

This man, having assured himself that Captain Smith seemed to be a discreet man who could keep his counsel and was ready for an adventure, proposed to charter the *Caledonia* for a voyage to the Ladrone Islands, in the North Pacific, in search of a treasure of which the secret was known to him alone. He offered 14,000 Mexican dollars for the charter of the *Caledonia.* It was a long voyage and far out of the schooner's usual beat but William Smith was a little tired of the peddling trade in which he had been engaged. It is true that the stranger did not have the 14,000 dollars in cash, but he had a persuasive way with him and he carried Captain Smith away with his talk of treasure. After all, 14,000 dollars was a deal of money.

Captain Roberton, as he called himself, seemed strangely out of place amongst the sealers and runaway convicts, the flotsam and jetsam of the islands of the Straits. He was a tall dark man with the air of command that suggested that he might have been a naval officer. He was hard-bitten and as reckless as the wildest amongst the sealers but he spoke a different language and had obviously been trained in a very different school. He had landed at Cape Barren from a whaling vessel that had come down from the whaling grounds of the North Pacific. When sober he was reserved with a forbidding look and a brooding air—in his cups he was moody and wildly excited by turns. It was noted that he often used Spanish oaths and snatches of Spanish at such times, though he was apparently of English or Scottish birth. However, he talked of liberal terms to Captain Smith who was ready for anything that promised profit. It was agreed that for the sum of 14,000 Mexican dollars Captain Smith should charter the *Caledonia* to Roberton for a voyage to an island in the Ladrones. Roberton would act as pilot while Smith would outfit the schooner for the voyage.

So Captain Smith slipped in Launceston to prepare for the long voyage. Roberton preferred to wait amongst the Straits men, fellows who asked no questions provided they had to answer none. Launceston itself was not the intensely respectable place that it has since become. The inhabitants were used to strange comings and goings and they knew Captain Smith and his schooner. No one was embarrassingly curious when he fitted out for a much longer voyage than those that he was accustomed to make.

Provisioned for a voyage to the North Pacific, the *Caledonia* cleared from Port Dalrymple, picked up Roberton at Cape Barren Island, stood away up the east coast of Australia, rounded the eastern end of New Guinea, worked through the maze of islands beyond and bore up for the Ladrones. It was a long voyage and a lazy one, once the schooner had run into the light airs and calms of the seas along the Line. The weather was pleasant, the provisions for the voyage had included plenty of rum and during the long tropic days Smith and his strange charterer drank together and talked of the sea, of treasures, and of what might be expected when they reached the isle whose secret Roberton held. Even Roberton began to mellow under the influence of the potent liquor of Launceston and dropped hints that the treasure of which he was in search was a huge one. Captain Smith's seasoned brain was also affected and these hints made him very scornful of a beggarly 14,000 dollars. After all he was providing the schooner and the crew and bearing all the expenses of the voyage.

As the *Caledonia* hung becalmed on the Equator the long smouldering bickerings burst into flame. One day, after a fierce quarrel, Roberton, a man of great strength as well as of a violent temper, knocked Captain Smith overboard. The quarrel had been embittered by the fact that the captain suspected Roberton of intriguing with the crew of the schooner. It was indeed the case that Roberton had been dangling before the eyes of some members of the crew the bait of wealth for themselves if they would follow him and abandon the captain. The majority of the *Caledonia*'s crew, however, would not see their Captain drown before their eyes. They lowered a boat and picked up Captain

Smith, sobered by his immersion and swearing vengeance on Roberton.

Yet the lure of the treasure was too strong. In imagination Captain Smith could see heaps of silver dollars, with gold and jewels, being dug out of the sands of a tropic isle. He saw himself, too, returning to Port Dalrymple to leave the sea and to live rich and respected. And Roberton held the clue to the treasure. So some sort of a peace was patched up and presently a breeze arose and carried the *Caledonia* northward towards the islands of the Ladrones.

Drunk or sober, Roberton kept his counsel about the exact point at which he was aiming but they were now amongst the innumerable islands of the Ladrone Group and it was to reach one of these that Roberton had chartered the *Caledonia*. Obviously the goal was not far off. Then, on a brilliant tropical morning, Captain Smith awoke from dreams of dollars to find that his best boat was missing. So was Roberton and several members of the crew. Captain Smith was a man who had ventured much in wild places and relied on his own strong right hand to secure justice and, if possible, a little more for himself. A man who could look after himself amongst the Straitsmen and with the wild savages and even wilder white men of the southern shores of Australia and of the north-east of Van Diemen's Land could be no weakling. Yet there was something hard, sinister and repellent about the swarthy scowling Roberton that chilled even Captain Smith. He was, too, in a region strange to him. Not far away, he knew, was the headquarters of Spanish rule in the Ladrones. And from stray hints of his earlier career when he had fought against the Spaniards, when the Spanish colonies of South America were striving to break loose from the mother country, Captain Smith guessed that the authorities would be willing enough to act against his charterer.

Blinded by anger and a touch of fear William Smith made a fatal mistake. He bore up for Guam and told his troubles to the Spanish Governor. That courteous official, Don Francisco Villalobos, Governor of the Ladrone and Marianne Islands, was full of sympathy and of understanding, when he found someone to interpret the complaints of this hard-faced captain who had dropped into Guam from some almost fabulous region in the far south. It was a scandalous thing that this scoundrel Roberton, a robber and an associate of rebels against his Majesty the King of Spain, should have plundered his benefactor. Action should at once be taken to have the ruffian brought to book.

Meanwhile there was one little irregularity about the proceedings of his visitor, for whom he professed undying regard, that must receive attention. He was indeed desolated to have to point out one thing to his friend Señor Smith. The *Caledonia* had entered the harbour of Guam in defiance of a law that no foreign vessel should put into the port without a licence from the King of Spain. These formalities were troublesome and it was natural enough for his friend Señor Smith to have overlooked them, yet they must be observed and he would most reluctantly be compelled to detain the schooner of Señor Smith till he could communicate with Manila.

Yet he begged his friend Señor Smith to be patient. The rascal Roberton would not be allowed to escape. He would send after him a fast sailing brig commanded by a most zealous and skilful officer, Don Francisco Miranda. Señor Smith had said something of a treasure supposed to be hidden amongst the islands. Don Miranda would attend to that little matter too.

So the *Caledonia* lay in Guam Harbour with Smith cursing Don Francisco Villalobos and all Spaniards for smooth rogues; and himself for a fool, while Miranda sailed in search of Roberton.

Miranda proved himself worthy of the praises of Don Francisco. Favoured by a fair wind he ran to the point where Roberton had left the *Caledonia* and after a little beating about amongst the islands came on Roberton and his associates still in the stolen boat. It was a dramatic meeting when Roberton was brought, a prisoner, on board the Spanish brig. He and Miranda had met before but then their positions had been reversed. Amongst many other episodes in a lurid past Roberton had fought under Lord Cochrane to free Chile from the yoke of Spain. Roberton had done good service for the "rebels", even if he may also have contrived to secure some pickings for himself. Miranda, as an officer in the Spanish Navy, had fought on the other side. He had been made a prisoner by Roberton who had had him soundly flogged. No wonder Miranda was exultant when he found out who the prisoner was. Many years had passed and they had wandered far apart but each knew the other on sight.

Roberton was brought before the Spanish captain on his quarter deck and told to reveal the whereabouts of the treasure. He refused to speak and was at once tied to the mast while two negro floggers, standing one on each side of him, and using their cat-o'-nine-tails alternately, gave him 300 strokes. Salt was then rubbed into his wounds and he was put into the hold to think over his stubbornness.

Next morning Roberton was again brought on deck. Again he refused to speak and the negro floggers laid on with right good will. After thirty strokes Roberton's iron resolution seemed to give way. He said that if he were sent in a boat he would guide the Spaniards to the treasure.

A boat was manned and Roberton was being lowered into it when he twisted out of the hands of the seamen who held him and disappeared into the sea. In the boat was a Manilaman, a professional diver. He went overboard after Roberton and brought him to the surface. But just as the seamen in the boat were reaching out their hands to haul him into the boat Roberton, with a last desperate effort, twisted himself out of the hands of the Manilaman and disappeared for ever.

Amongst Roberton's few possessions they found a rough map of an island with all the conventional treasure island marks. There was the lone palm tree and the cross marking the location of the treasure. Miranda hunted around and amongst the islands of the Ladrone group but Roberton had carried his secret to the sea-bottom with him and if there was any treasure it was never found.

Yet inquiries suggested that Captain Roberton had told William Smith the truth when he hinted at riches lying hidden on some desert island. It was found that some years before Roberton had sailed from Callao for Manila on a vessel carrying 90,000 dollars and other treasure. The vessel never reached Manila and was supposed to have been lost at sea with all hands. Piecing together what he learned from the ever courteous Spaniards with what Roberton had told him, Captain Smith came to the conclusion that Roberton had contrived to scuttle the vessel or run it ashore on some outlying island of the Ladrone group, and that with the help of some confederates he had made away with those survivors who were not in the secret, on the principle that dead men tell no tales, and buried the treasure. After that he had contrived, who knew by what mixture of treachery and of ferocity, to rid himself of those who had assisted him. Then he had drifted southward till he had fallen in with Captain Smith and his handy schooner at Cape Barren Island.

When the Spaniards had satisfied themselves that the treasure for which Roberton had bartered his soul was not to be found, the Governor, with many bows, and apologies, assured his good but rather impatient friend Señor Smith, that the authorities at Manila were prepared to overlook that trifling breach of regulations, in view of the unusual circumstances, and that the *Caledonia* was free to depart whither she would. The Governor also expressed himself as most happy to be able, owing to the exertions of his faithful officer Don Miranda, to return to Señor Smith the ship's boat of the *Caledonia* which that accursed scoundrel and murderer Roberton had stolen from him.

William Smith was a plain blunt man or he might, as the *Caledonia* pulled out of Guam Harbour and started on the long run across the Line and down to Bass Straits, have thought of the words of Robinson Crusoe: "Dangers as well of the seas as of the Japanese who are a false cruel and treacherous people and of the Spaniards of the Philippines, more false cruel and treacherous than they."

He was returning empty-handed, with nothing to show for a voyage of nearly 10,000 miles, and would have to take up again the slow business of working in and out of Port Dalrymple, of beating to and fro amongst the treacherous tides and strong gales of Bass Straits, with its rocks and sunken reefs, carrying to Launceston cargoes of sealskins, wattlebark and oil in place of the gold and silver of which he had dreamed. Gone was the vision of retiring from the sea to a house in Launceston or an estate in the country where he would live a respected citizen of wealth and of position.

Yet as he remembered the cold eye and the deadly violence of the swarthy Roberton and eked out the story of the vessel that put out across the Pacific with the dark hints of horror that Roberton let fall when they drank together in equatorial calms, perhaps he was glad that he had not found the treasure but was at least returning safe and sound while Roberton slept beneath the tropic seas.

THOMAS DUNBABIN

CAPTAIN BLIGH

Living on the side of the Pacific, or at least beside one remote corner of that great ocean, the story of Captain Bligh and the mutiny in the barque *Bounty* was real to us. Bligh, after all, had been one of the early Governors of New South Wales at a time when this included also my home state of Victoria. He had had a mutiny there, too, but in that case at any rate, the weight of local sympathy was with him. He found some "rackets" and tried to clear them up, and the military clique in Sydney was too strong for him. That was about all there was to the so-called Rum Rebellion in New South Wales. A far greater seaman than poor Bligh got into trouble trying to disturb a racket once, when Nelson found a queer smell round some of the West Indian Islands. Nelson was not the Governor, and could not clear things up too much, which was probably as well for him at that stage of his career.

One day in Coles Book Arcade—useful place, though the prices were a little higher than those in the Victoria Market —I came upon an interesting old book. It was called *A Narrative of the "Briton's" Voyage to Pitcairn's Island, etc., etc.*, by Lieut. J. Shillibeer, R.M., printed in London in 1817. Somebody had had the copy rebound and it cost a shilling, which was a lot of money to me. However, I bought it (with funds earned on a newspaper round). I was very glad I did, for the book contained an interesting account of an early visit to the surviving *Bounty* mutineers found on Pitcairn. These South Sea islands seemed to me pretty good places to sail to when I got the chance.

Bligh and his *Bounty* were of the stuff of high adventure to me—the *real* stuff, on my doorstep. I always preferred the real to the concocted. I lapped it up.

Here it is:

At Pitcairn's Island

Having sailed from the Marquesas, it will be necessary for me to take a cursory view of Mr Bligh's voyage to Otaheite, in 1788, about which period he was appointed to the command of the *Bounty*, with a Mr Christian as his Chief Mate, or First Lieutenant, for the purpose of conveying the bread-fruit tree to the West Indies. The progress he made in his undertaking—his sailing from Otaheite—the subsequent mutiny—the entire annihilation of the object of his voyage, and the miraculous return to the coast of Timor, in an open boat, are circumstances so well known, and have been so feelingly described, that at the very name of the *Bounty*, they must recur with such strength to any reflective mind, that it will be needless for me to touch on the conduct of the unfortunate young man, who led that much to be lamented conspiracy, or that of the experienced Navigator, who appears to have been the chief object of their hatred, and I am afraid the sole cause of the unjustifiable conduct used towards him.

The full-rigged ship *Joseph Conrad* was the Danish school-ship *Georg Stage* when I bought her in 1934. A single topsail ship of the old school, she was only 400 tons—ideal for the lads for whom she was designed. I hoped to make her a British school-ship, but there was no support for the idea. The photograph was made in the Sargasso Sea as the beautiful ship stood silent in her own image, courses hauled up to prevent them slatting to pieces. She is preserved at Mystic, Connecticut, U.S.A.

Looking aloft at the massive strength of one of the last of the Cape Horners, the 3000-ton four-masted barque *Parma*. Steel masts, steel yards, iron-wire standing rigging, much of the running rigging also wire, she is designed to use high winds, to seek them wherever they may usefully be found and convert them by the machinery of these sails and rigging into power to drive her where she may be bound

Swift-running four-master, a bowsprit view taken aboard the *Parma* between the Horn and the Falkland Islands in 1933. Under all sail with a "soldier's wind" in a quiet sea, she runs in ideal conditions. Net below the bowsprit is for saving sails and crew, when the vessel dips her bows into a sea. Note that even the buntlines are wire—the lines on the sails. This passage we came from Spencer Gulf in 83 days

Typical of the last of the big steel "Windjammers", the four-masted barque *Parma* lolling in a Horse latitudes calm, between the Westerlies and the Trades. Built on the Clyde in 1902 as the *Arrow*, the 3084-ton sailer was later sold to the famous Hamburg House of Laeisz for the Chilean nitrate trade—one of the hardest in the world. A small syndicate, in which I had 16/64th shares, bought her for the Australian grain trade in 1931. She loaded just over 5200 tons, carried a crew of 24 under the Finnish flag

Above
Fat decks of enormous oil-tanker, queerly named *Universe Apollo*, are filled with pipe-lines, tank-tops, pump connections to facilitate rapid oil-handling. *Universe Apollo*'s 27,500 shaft horse power gave her better than 17½ knots on trials. In the 1960s, oil-tankers of over 100,000 tons displacement have been built

Below
Night scene at Hay's Wharf, London, where the short sea traders congregate in the world's greatest port. Cluster lights facilitate cargo work by night to permit quick turn-round

Photographs by Fox Photos

Fox Photos

Yachting at Cowes—along the sunlit, flattened water the big yachts glide with grace, neck and neck, like racehorses in the straight. Big spinnakers fill handsomely, alert crews watch trim and set. Beautiful, fast, such yachts are not for £200 "millionaires" like Weston Martyr: any of them, with a snugger rig, could sail round the world

official R.N. photograph

Above: Ships of two widely differing ages—the Royal Navy's huge carrier *Ark Royal* salutes the little *Mayflower II* on a quiet day at sea. Replica of the Pilgrim Fathers' *Mayflower*, the new ship sailed from Plymouth, England, to Plymouth, Massachusetts, in 53 days in 1957

Below: Aboard an ocean-racing yacht, Dr Pedro Theotonio Pereira's schooner *Bellatrix*, running in a high sea across the Bay of Biscay from Tor Bay to Lisbon. Such ocean races now are commonplace, as yachts take the place of sailing-ships

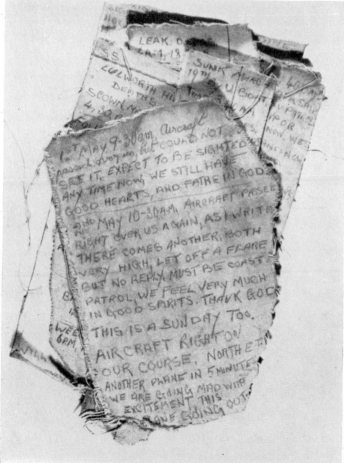

Above

A miraculous raft voyage of the Second World War—torpedoed ship's carpenter Kenneth Cooke, G.M., and able seaman Colin Armitage bring their frail craft alongside rescuing destroyer *Rapid* after 50 days adrift at sea. They cling to their masts to keep on their feet, had to be carried aboard

Left

Cooke kept a log on bits of canvas—all he had. These are pieces of his astonishing log. Though 14 others died, he never lost his faith or spirits

photographs by courtesy of Imperial War Museum

For many years, the ultimate fate of Christian was uncertain'
and the prevailing opinion was, that after he had left and destroyed
the *Bounty*, he returned to the coast of South America, and
entered into the Spanish service; nay, it has even been asserted,
he had been recognized in that situation, and after the account
given of him by Mayhew Folgier,* there were many who retained
the same opinion; but the matter is at present too clearly demonstrated to admit of a doubt, and those idle tales must now meet
the fate they then merited.

The following account is given in the Missionary Voyage,
of the conduct of the Mutineers at, and their departure from
Otaheite, since which period to the time of Captain Folgier's
touching at Pitcairn's, every thing relative to those infatuated
men had been but a vague conjecture.

"The wind blew fresh from Toubouai, and the intention of our
Captain was not to go near this Island; but for the sake of some
who were desirous of seeing it, we tacked to windward, and
towards evening got within a few miles of it; he thought it not
prudent to land on account of the natives being prejudiced
against the English, through the Mutineers of the *Bounty*, who
had destroyed near a hundred of them.

"This Island was discovered by Captain Cook, in the year 1777,
and upon it the unhappy Fletcher Christian, with his companions,
the Mutineers of the *Bounty*, attempted a settlement in 1789. They
had with them some natives of Otaheite, and live stock of different sorts. Notwithstanding the opposition they met with from
the natives on their first arrival, they warped the ship through the
only opening in the reef; then landed, chose a spot of ground,
built a fort thereon, and taking their live stock on shore, they
intended, had the natives proved friendly to their stay, to have destroyed the *Bounty* and fixed themselves there: but their own
unruly conduct alienated the natives from them, who withheld
their women, which they were ready to seize by violence: they
excited the jealousy of the chiefs by a friendship formed with one
in preference to the rest; they were disunited amongst themselves,
and many longed for Otaheite: they resolved to leave Toubouai,
and carry with them all the live stock which they had brought,
the benefit of which the Toubouians began to understand, and
were unwilling to see them again all collected and removed. This
caused the first brawl between the Otaheitean servants, who were
driving in the hogs, and the natives. Insolence, and want of
gentleness, and conciliation, led to all the bloody consequences

* The master of the first ship which touched at Pitcairn's Island.

57

which ensued. The natives were numerous, and fought with great courage, forcing the Mutineers, to avail themselves of a high ground, where with their superior skill, and the advantage of fire-arms, and the aid of the Otaheiteans, who fought bravely on this occasion, they at last came off victorious, with only two of themselves wounded, whilst the dead bodies of the Toubouians covered the spot; and were afterwards thrown up in three or four heaps. Thus finding that no peaceable settlement was now to be obtained in this place, they shipped their live stock, abandoned their fort, and taking their friendly chief on board with them, weighed anchor and steered towards Mātavāi bay, in the Island of Otaheite. On their passage thither it is said Christian became very melancholy, confining himself to his cabin, and would hardly speak a word to any person; lamenting most probably, that the resolutions he had formed without deliberation, and executed with rash haste, had now involved his life, and those of his adherents in misery. As soon as they anchored in Mātavāi bay in Otaheite, those who wished to stay there went on shore; but nine of the Mutineers, and also some of the native men and women remained on board. With these, Christian cutting the cable in the night, put to sea, and steering to the N.W. has never been heard of since."

We left the friendly Marquesans on the 2d of September, and were proceeding on our voyage to regain the port of Valparaiso, steering a course which ought, according to the charts and every other authority, to have carried us nearly 3 degrees of longitude to the eastward of Pitcairn's Island, and our surprize was greatly excited by its sudden and unexpected appearance. It was in the second watch when we made it. At day light, we proceeded to a more close examination, and soon perceived huts, cultivation, and people; of the latter, some were making signs, others launching their little canoes through the surf, into which they threw themselves with great dexterity, and pulled towards us.

At this moment I believe neither Captain Bligh (of the *Bounty*), nor Christian, had entered any of our thoughts, and in waiting for approach of the strangers, we prepared to ask them some questions in the language of those people we had so recently left. They came—and for me to picture the wonder which was conspicuous in every countenance, at being hailed in perfect English, what was the name of the ship, and who commanded her, would be impossible—our surprize can alone be conceived. The Captain answered, and now a regular conversation commenced. He requested them to come alongside, and the reply was, "We have no boathook to hold on by." "I will throw you a rope," said the Captain. "If you do we have nothing to make it fast to," was the answer. However, they at length came on board, exemplifying not the least fear, but their astonishment was unbounded.

After the friendly salutation of "Good morrow Sir", from the first man who entered, (Mackey) for that was his name, "Do you know", said he, "one William Bligh, in England?" This question threw a new light on the subject, and he was immediately asked if he knew one Christian, and the reply was given with so much natural simplicity, that I shall here use his proper words. "Oh yes," said he, "very well, his son is in the boat there coming up, his name is Friday Fletcher October Christian. His father is dead now—he was shot by a black fellow." Several of them had now reached the ship, and the scene was become exceedingly interesting, every one betrayed the greatest anxiety to know the ultimate fate of that misled young man, of whose end so many vague reports had been in circulation, and those who did not ask questions, devoured with avidity every word which led to an elucidation of the mysterious termination of the unfortunate *Bounty*.

The questions which were now put were numerous, and as I am inclined to believe their being arranged with their specific answers, will convey to the reader, the circumstance as it really took place, with greater force than a continued relation, I shall adopt that plan, and those occurrences which did not lead immediately to the end of Christian, and the establishment of the colony, I will relate faithfully as they transpired.

Question.—Christian you say was shot?

Answer.—Yes he was.

Q.—By whom?

A.—A black fellow shot him.

Q.—What cause do you assign for the murder?

A.—I know no reason, except a jealousy which I have heard then existed between the people of Otaheite and the English—Christian was shot in the back while at work in his yam plantation.

Q.—What became of the man who killed him?

A.—Oh! that black fellow was shot afterwards by an Englishman.

Q.—Was there any other disturbance between the Otaheiteans and English, after the death of Christian?

A.—Yes, the black fellows rose, shot two Englishmen, and wounded John Adams, who is now the only remaining man who came in the *Bounty*.

Q.—How did Adams escape being murdered?

A.—He hid himself in the wood, and the same night, the

women enraged at the murder of the English to whom they were more partial than their countrymen, rose and put every Otaheitean to death in their sleep. This saved Adams, his wounds were soon healed, and although old, he now enjoys good health.

Q.—How many men and women did Christian bring with him in the *Bounty*?

A.—Nine white men, six from Otaheite, and eleven women.

Q.—And how many are there now on the Island?

A.—In all we have 48.

Q.—Have you ever heard Adams say how long it is since he came to the Island?

A.—I have heard it is about 25 years ago.

Q.—And what became of the *Bounty*?

A.—After every thing useful was taken out of her, she was run on shore, set fire to, and burnt.

Q.—Have you ever heard how many years it is since Christian was shot?

A.—I understand it was about two years after his arrival at the Island.

Q.—What became of Christian's wife?

A.—She died soon after Christian's son was born, and I have heard that Christian took forcibly the wife of one of the black fellows to supply her place, and which was the chief cause of his being shot.

Q.—Then Fletcher October Christian is the oldest on the Island, except John Adams, and the old women?

A.—Yes, he is the first born on the Island.

Q.—At what age do you marry?

A.—Not before 19 or 20.

Q.—Are you allowed to have more than one wife?

A.—No! we can have but one, and it is wicked to have more.

Q.—Have you been taught any religion?

A.—Yes, a very good religion.

Q.—In what do you believe?

A.—I believe in God the Father Almighty, &c. (Here he went through the whole of the Belief.)

Q.—Who first taught you this Belief?

A.—John Adams says it was first by F. Christian's order, and that he likewise caused a prayer to be said every day at noon.

Q.—And what is the prayer?

A.—It is,—"I will arise and go to my Father, and say unto him, Father, I have sinned against Heaven, and before thee, and am no more worthy of being called thy son."

Q.—Do you continue to say this every day?

A.—Yes, we never neglect it.

Q.—What language do you commonly speak?

A.—Always English.

Q.—But you understand the Otaheitean?

A.—Yes, but not so well.

Q.—Do the old women speak English?

A.—Yes, but not so well as they understand it, their pronunciation is not good.

Q.—What countrymen do you call yourselves?

A.—Half English, and half Otaheite.

Q.—Who is your King?

A.—Why, King George to be sure.

Q.—Have you ever seen a ship before?

A.—Yes, we have seen four from the Island, but only one stopped. Mayhew Folgier was the Captain, I suppose you know him?—No, we do not know him.

Q.—How long did he stay?

A.—Two days.

Q.—Should you like to go to England?

A.—No! I cannot, I am married, and have a family.

Before we had finished our interrogatories the hour of breakfast had arrived, and we solicited our half countrymen, as they styled themselves, to accompany us below, and partake of our repast, to which they acquiesced without much ceremony. The circle in which we had surrounded them being opened, brought to the notice of Mackey, a little black terrier. He was at first frightened, ran behind one of the officers, and looking over his shoulder said, pointing to the dog, "I know what that is, it is a dog, I never saw a dog before—will it bite?" After a short pause he addressed himself to Christian, saying with great admiration, "It is a pretty thing too to look at, is it not?"

The whole of them were inquisitive, and in their questions as well as answers, betrayed a very great share of natural abilities.

They asked the names of whatever they saw, and the purposes to which it was applied. This, they would say, was pretty,—that they did not like, and were greatly surprised at our having so many things which they were not possessed of in the Island.

The circumstance of the dog, the things which at each step drew their attention or created their wonder, retarded us on our road to the breakfast table, but arriving there, we had a new cause for surprize. The astonishment which before had been so strongly demonstrated in them, was now become conspicuous in us, even to a much greater degree than when they hailed us in our native language; and I must here confess I blushed when I saw nature in its most simple state, offer that tribute of respect to the Omnipotent Creator, which from education I did not perform, nor from society had been taught its necessity. Before they began to eat; on their knees, and with hands uplifted did they implore permission to partake in peace what was set before them, and when they had eaten heartily, resuming their former attitude, offered a fervent prayer of thanksgiving for the indulgence they had just experienced. Our omission of this ceremony did not escape their notice, for Christian asked me whether it was not customary with us also. Here nature was triumphant, for I should do myself an irreparable injustice, did I not with candour acknowledge, I was both embarrassed and wholly at a loss for a sound reply, and evaded this poor fellow's question by drawing his attention to the cow, which was then looking down the hatchway, and as he had never seen any of the species before, it was a source of mirth and gratification to him.

The hatred of these people to the blacks is strongly rooted, and which doubtless owes its origin to the early quarrels which Christian and his followers had with the Otaheiteans after their arrival at Pitcairn's; to illustrate which I shall here relate an occurrence which took place at breakfast.

Soon after young Christian had began, a West Indian Black, who was one of the servants, entered the gun-room to attend table as usual. Christian looked at him sternly, rose, asked for his hat, and said, "I don't like that black fellow, I must go," and it required some little persuasion, before he would again resume his seat. The innocent Quashe was often reminded of the anecdote by his fellow servants.

After coming along side the ship, so eager were they to get on board, that several of the canoes had been wholly abandoned, and gone adrift. This was the occasion of an anecdote which will show most conspicuously the good nature of their dispositions, and the mode resorted to in deciding a double claim. The canoes being brought back to the ship, the Captain ordered that one of them should remain in each, when it became a question to which that duty should devolve; however it was soon adjusted, for Mackey observed that he supposed they were all equally anxious to see the ship, and the fairest way would be for them to cast lots, as then there would be no ill will on either side. This was acceded to, and those to whom it fell to go into the boat, departed without a murmur.

I could wish it had been possible for us to have prolonged our stay for a few days, not only for our own gratification, but for the benefit which these poor people would have derived from it, for I am perfectly satisfied, from the interest every one took, nothing would have been withheld by the lowest of the crew which probability told him would add to their comfort: however this was impossible; for, from some cause on the part of the commissariat department, and which I cannot well explain, we were reduced to so comparatively small a portion of provisions, that it was necessary to use every means to expedite our return to South America, and after ascertaining the longitude to be in 130°25', W. and latitude 25°4' S. we again set sail and proceeded on our voyage.

No one but the Captain went ashore, which will be a source of lasting regret to me, for I would rather have seen the simplicity of that little village, than all the splendour and magnificence of a city.

I now lament it the more, because the conclusion of this chapter will be from the relation of another, and I was willing to lay as little as possible before the reader, but what I had myself been a witness; still, as I can rely on its veracity, I shall hope it will please. "After landing," said my friend, "and we had ascended a little eminence, we were imperceptibly led through groups of cocoa-nuts and bread-fruit trees, to a beautiful picturesque little village, formed on an oblong square, with trees of various kinds irregularly interspersed. The houses small, but regular, convenient, and of unequalled cleanliness. The daughter of Adams received us on the hill. She came doubtlessly as a spy, and had we taken men, or even been armed ourselves, would certainly have given her father timely notice to escape, but as we had neither, she waited our arrival, and conducted us to where her father was. She was arrayed in nature's simple garb and wholly unadorned, but she was beauty's self, and needed not the aid of ornament. She betrayed some surprize—timidity was a prominent feature.

"John Adams is a fine looking old man, approaching to sixty years of age. We conversed with him a long time, relative to the mutiny of the *Bounty*, and the ultimate fate of Christian. He denied being accessory to, or having the least knowledge of the conspiracy, but he expressed great horror at the conduct of Captain Bligh, not only towards his men, but officers also. I asked him if he had a desire to return to England, and I must confess his replying in the affirmative, caused me great surprize.

"He told me he was perfectly aware how deeply he was involved; that by following the fortune of Christian, he had not only sacrificed every claim to his country, but that his life was the necessary forfeiture for such an act, and he supposed would be exacted from him was he ever to return: not-withstanding all these circumstances, nothing would be able to occasion him so much gratification as that of seeing once more, prior to his death, that country which gave him birth, and from which he had been so long estranged.

"There was a sincerity in his speech, I can badly describe it— but it had a very powerful influence in persuading me these were his real sentiments. My interest was excited to so great a degree, that I offered him a conveyance for himself, with any of his family who chose to accompany him. He appeared pleased at the proposal, and as no one was then present, he sent for his wife and children. The rest of this little community surrounded the door. He communicated his desire, and solicited their acquiescence. Appalled at a request not less sudden than in opposition to their wishes, they were all at a loss for a reply.

"His charming daughter although inundated with tears, first broke the silence.

" 'Oh do not, Sir,' said she, 'take from me my father! do not take away my best—my dearest friend.' Her voice failed her— she was unable to proceed—leaned her head upon her hand, and gave full vent to her grief. His wife too (an Otaheitean) expressed a lively sorrow. The wishes of Adams soon became known among the others, who joined in pathetic solicitation for his stay on the Island. Not an eye was dry—the big tear stood in those of the men—the women shed them in full abundance. I never wit-nessed a scene so fully affecting, or more replete with interest. To have taken him from a circle of such friends, would have ill become a feeling heart, to have forced him away in opposition to their joint and earnest entreaties, would have been an outrage on humanity.

"With assurances that it was neither our wish nor intention to take him from them against his inclination, their fears were at length dissipated. His daughter too had gained her usual serenity, but she was lovely in her tears, for each seemed to add an addi-tional charm. Forgetting the unhappy deed which placed Adams in that spot, and seeing him only in the character he now is, at the head of a little community, adored by all, instructing all, in religion, industry, and friendship, his situation might be truly envied, and one is almost inclined to hope that his unremitting attention to the government and morals of this extraordinary little colony, will ultimately prove an equivalent for the part he formerly took,—entitle him to praise, and should he ever return to England, ensure him the clemency of that Sovereign he has so much injured.

"The young women have invariably beautiful teeth, fine eyes, and open expression of countenance, and looks of such simple innocence, and sweet sensibility, that renders their appearance at once interesting and engaging, and it is pleasing to add, their minds and manners were as pure and innocent, as this impression indicated. No lascivious looks, or any loose, forward manners, which so much distinguish the characters of the females of the other Islands."

The Island itself has an exceedingly pretty appearance, and I was informed by Christian, every part was fertile and capable of being cultivated. The coast is every way bound with rocks, inso-much that they are at all times obliged to carry their little boast to the village, but the timber is of so light a nature that one man is adequate to the burden of the largest they have.

Each family has a separate allotment of land, and each strives to rival the other in their agricultural pursuits, which is chiefly confined to the propagation of the Yam, and which they have certainly brought to the finest perfection I ever saw. The bread-fruit and cocoa-nut trees, were brought with them in the *Bounty*, and have been since reared with great success. The pigs also came by the same conveyance, as well as goats and poultry. They had no pigeons, and I am sorry to say no one thought of leaving those few we had on board, with them.

The pigs have got into the woods, and many are now wild. Fish of various sorts are taken here, and in great abundance; the tackling is all of their own manufacturing, and the hooks, although beat out of old iron hoops, not only answer the purpose, but are fairly made.

Needles they also make from the same materials. Those men who came on board, were finely formed, and of manly features. Their height about 5 feet 10 inches. Their hair black and long, generally plaited into a tail.

They wore a straw hat, similar to those worn by sailors, with a few feathers stuck into them by way of ornament. On their shoulders was a mantle resembling the Chilian Poncho, which hung down to the knee, and round the waist, a girdle corres-ponding to that of the Indians at the Marquesas, both of which are produced from the bark of trees growing on the Island. They told me they had clothes on shore, but never wore them. I spoke to Christian particularly, of Adams, who assured me he was greatly

65

respected, insomuch that no one acted in opposition to his wishes, and when they should lose him, their regret would be general. The inter-marriages which had taken place among them, have been the occasion of a relationship throughout the colony. There seldom happens to be a quarrel, even of the most trivial nature, and then (using their own term) is nothing more than a word of mouth quarrel, which is always referred to Adams for adjustment.

SOME PACIFIC WRECKS

There were plenty of wrecks in the days of sail, and there were icebergs, reefs, and islands enough to rip the bottoms out of ships in the Pacific Ocean, even on the long, lonely road that stretched from Melbourne and Sydney towards Cape Horn. As a boy, I became used to brief paragraphs in the Shipping Columns of the Melbourne *Age* and *Argus* announcing that such and such a splendid ship had failed to arrive or to be reported anywhere. After a certain time, she was posted Missing—entered in a special book at Lloyd's as a vessel untraced—and her insurance paid over.

Sometimes, but not often, news of such ships was received again. Some of them were wrecked on the few sub-Antarctic islands in the Roaring Forties, the Aucklands and Campbell Island. There was plenty of sea-room, the Lord knows, but a few ships hit the islands. (Establishing longitude was a problem, of course. Most sailing-ships carried only one chronometer and there were no radio checks then. In the Cape Horners I served, at least we tried to keep on a safe latitude always—any latitude *not* that of dangers. Latitude was more easily established, but even that required a noon look at the sun and a checked compass. Most masters did not bother with star sights, and masters were generally the only navigators. They owned the few charts aboard and guarded them like gold.)

The losses of the four-masted barque *Dundonald* and the *General Grant* on the Auckland Islands were well-remembered tragedies in my youth. At least there were some survivors from both of them.

The well-known sailing-ship historian Basil Lubbock

gives the bare bones of their stories. (Lubbock was at sea as a youth in the four-masted barque *Ross-shire*, a passage-worker home from San Francisco after the Klondyke gold rush, and maintained a lifelong interest afterwards in sailing-ships. It was a good thing he did, for few others then bothered about their records and it is too late now—it was too late indeed by 1930.)

Mr Lubbock wastes no words. Here is his account of the loss of the *General Grant*:

The *General Grant*, a passenger ship of 1,200 tons, left Melbourne on May 4, 1866, with £10,000 worth of gold dust, 12 saloon and 33 first and second class passengers.

On the night of May 13 she drifted up against the perpendicular cliffs of Auckland Island in a calm. The first crash carried away the jibboom. She was then carried stern first by the current for about half a mile to another projecting rock. This time she lost her spanker boom and rudder, and the wheel in spinning round broke the ribs of the helmsman. This collision canted the ship's head into a huge cave about 250 yards long. As the *General Grant* was swept into the cave on the top of a swell, the foremast struck the roof and was carried away close to the deck. The main topgallant-mast followed it. Large rocks also fell from the roof and stove in the forecastle-head.

For the rest of the night the ship lay bumping and crashing against the roof and walls of this awful cavern, until at last her mainmast was driven through her bottom and she began to sink. The boats were hurriedly lowered but were nearly all capsized in the surf, only ten survivors, including the stewardess, getting safely ashore. Captain Loughlin, when last seen, was waving his hand to the boats from the mizzen top. The *General Grant* sank ten minutes later and took her commander down with her.

After being on the island for 18 months the castaways were eventually rescued by the *Amherst* (Captain Gilroy) from Bluff, New Zealand. Since that date many attempts have been made to salvage the treasure from the *General Grant*, but although a few pieces of wreckage were found, no diver has ever located any of the gold.

BASIL LUBBOCK: *Last of the Windjammers*

Lubbock does scant justice to the story. There were wrecks enough among the last of the windjammers, certainly, but the dreadful agony of the gold-carrying ship, pounding herself to pieces in the only cave that would hold her upon the whole savage Cape Horn road, smashing and grinding there in Stygian gloom until the stump of her own mainmast hammered through her bottom and sent her down, surely deserves a better account.

Of all the fates that ever overtook a ship, this must be the strangest. That any of her people survived at all is extraordinary. It was winter when the *Grant* blew into the cave. The only way out was to go back to sea. The wind had risen, after she grounded, and the surf was an absolute maelstrom. The only way to launch boats was to let them float off the main-deck as a surging sea swept the ship. Rocks falling as the mastheads scraped the inside of the cave-top added to the difficulties. Passengers and crew took refuge under the break of the poop. When they got a longboat off, it capsized. The only boat that did get away and out of the cave fetched up on another rock, for it was impossible to land by night. The cave was in a perpendicular wall of rock 400 feet high. By daylight, the few survivors were able to scramble ashore elsewhere on the island. It was a grim and storm-swept place. All it offered in the way of food were seals and seabirds, alike unpalatable. Later they found some wild goats, and a rough hut left by some previous castaways.

Here they lived for eighteen months. They might have died there were it not for the courage and ingenuity of an Irish seaman named Jack Teer. He made many messages scratched on pieces of wood and tied to seal bladders, which he blew up, and sent off in the sea. But the seabirds thought these a new sort of food and punctured them, causing them to sink. Then he carved minute boats and attached small zinc sails to them with a message scratched on, requesting help for the castaways. The seabirds could neither eat nor sink these. One day a sail was seen making towards the island, but it turned away when close.

At this, four of the survivors, unable to bear further disappointments—with the consent of the others—launched the only boat and sailed off to try to reach New Zealand. Nothing of these was heard again. Teer stayed on with the rest. Scurvy attacked them.

At last, on November 21, 1867, the whaling brig *Amherst* stood in to the roadstead off the island. Her captain had picked up one of the little boats. (Whalemen kept a sharp lookout.) Yet even then, the tragedy was not ended. Taking a look at the desperate, wild and hair-covered sub-humans who clamoured to be taken aboard his ship, Captain Gilroy of the *Amherst* suddenly had the frightful suspicion that they might be escaped convicts. There *were* such parties about. He had heard of them among the islands further north, where they had seized ships. The *Amherst* had been too long at sea to have heard of the missing *General Grant*, even though the ship had been gone from Melbourne then over a year and a half.

So he would not allow the scurvy-stricken, half-starved and now also half-crazed wretches to come aboard.

They would have been compelled to go back to their island to die there. But the extraordinary Teer saved them again, by a most astonishing coincidence.

"Good God!" he shouted. "There's my old shipmate Sawny Bill! Hey, Bill! Bill! Don't you remember me?"

Bill, one of the *Amherst*'s crew, taking a long look, did.

And so the *Grant*'s people were saved, and taken away in due course, back to Melbourne.

If it was odd indeed that the *General Grant* should thread herself into the only cave she could have found, it was almost odder that Able Seaman Teer should recognise a shipmate in the only ship which came to her rescue there.

THE "MISSIONARY" BRIG CARL

When I was a little older, and on the rare occasions that I was ashore in my home port between ships, I liked to browse in the old newspaper files in the Public Library of Melbourne. Naturally, I concentrated on their Shipping Columns, which were always interesting. There used to be a special breed of newspaper-man who specialised in ships and their stories. He boarded incoming vessels and got their news—such as it might be—and recorded this accurately, and usually at a decent length, in special columns (frequently extended to a column and a half or even two columns) in our respected *Age* and *Argus*. He had to be accurate, for he was catering for a wide audience which knew ships, and generally took a passionate interest in them. New clippers and emigrant ships were described in detail (after a good lunch aboard, I don't doubt): now and again more sombre matters came to notice.

Sometimes these spread over into the Police Court Proceedings, like the criminal proceedings which arose out of the murders aboard the brig *Carl*. Murder, in some form or other, aboard a South Seas brig was not so ¦strange, but the *Carl* had pretended to be a missionary vessel, the cold-blooded murder by her people of defenceless Kanakas in the Solomon Islands led directly to the retaliatory murder of several missionaries, and the *Carl* had begun her voyage from Melbourne. Under charter to a fiend named Murray, she sailed for the Islands (as the South Pacific groups were always known to us) from Melbourne on June 8, 1871—the middle of winter there. She cleared for what was called a "labour" cruise. The waterfront term for this was black-birding. The police word was murder.

Two seamen stood trial at Melbourne's City Police Court in December 1872. Charterer Murray was allowed to turn Queen's evidence. The charge was wilful murder. The Crown Prosecutor, in his opening address, declared that while the brig was under easy sail canoes were lured alongside by the pretence that the brig belonged to a missionary society. The evidence, he said, would show "the manner in which these canoes were sunk by pig iron and small cannon attached to rope being lowered precipitously down the ship's side into them, upsetting them; how while in the water the natives were seized and, if any resistance was offered, they were knocked on the head with oars or sling-shot or clubs; how at Buka some 80 natives were seized and put into the vessel, and how they resisted and made efforts to regain their liberty; how those on board the *Carl* fired at intervals during the whole night into the hold of the vessel until in the morning it was found that about 70 natives were killed or wounded; how in the morning the dead were brought on deck with the dying, some of them tied, and thrown overboard, all of them, those that were dead with those that were dying. . . ."

From the evidence of George Heath, a seaman in the *Carl*, the following may be extracted:

We went cruising to several islands until we came to Bougainville, where canoes came off in great numbers. The canoes were capsized by means of cannon and pig iron dropped into them, and the natives seized. There was a good deal of resistance every time at Bougainville. Somewhere about eighty-five natives were taken and they were all put into the hold. The hold was then very crowded, and there was just room for the natives to lie down. After filling the hold we put to sea, and the first night the natives were noisy. They were told to be quiet, but no shot was fired this night. The next night there was more noise. The natives had armed themselves with poles which were got in Apia to lay fore and aft as bunks for sleeping in. They had broken these up and were trying to force the hatchway. All hands then commenced firing down the hatchway. No natives came out. They could not. This firing continued on and off during the night from half-past ten till daylight. Mount shone a bull's eye through the hatch and the others shot. In the morning Mr Scott tried to go down the hatchway, but was repulsed by the natives with poles. He came up, went aft, and with Dr Murray—the charterer of the ship— went down the fore cabin. Here they bored holes with augers in the bulkhead and fired at the natives again through these. This was in the morning, and went on for about half-an-hour. Then a ladder was lowered into the hold, and those of the natives who could walk came up it. They did not offer to do anything then. They were all wounded, and blood-covered. Only about 10 would come up. They were more dead than alive. Dr Murray picked out a few who would recover quickly and ordered them to be kept, and ordered the other natives to be thrown overboard. They were thrown overboard. Some of those who were thrown overboard were alive. Some could stand and some could talk. Some were tied. Some of the natives crawled to the side when they saw the others thrown overboard, and jumped over themselves. . . .

In the course of his evidence Heath describes Murray's attempt at making the *Carl* a missionary ship:

. . . At one of the islands, about seven miles from Apia, the captain wanted the natives to come off but they would not, and while they were laughing and chaffing in the cabin Murray said "This is a big ship; I think the best thing we can do is to dress up as missionaries." They were to disguise the ship as if she had been a missionary ship. They did disguise her, and the captain put on the mate's monkey jacket turned inside out, the inside being red, and took a book under his arm. The mate was disguised and did not have his usual ship rig. Dr Murray got a rug and put it over Wilson's shoulders and pinned it behind. Mount put on a red dressing gown, a smoking cap, and a Chinese umbrella and Chinese slippers, and was knocking about the decks that way with a book under his arm. A seaman named Mick disguised himself with white duck trousers and a blue serge shirt which he had got from some one. Then two Kanakas who had shipped at Fiji as part of the regular crew pulled them all ashore, where they went to the natives, giving out leaves from the books as tracts. . . .

Police Court Proceedings, Melbourne, December 1872

Blackbirders, pirates, beachcombers, seafaring hoodlums roamed the South Seas. They were a colourful lot, especially in retrospect. I barely managed to catch the very last of this era. A federated Commonwealth of Australia, from the time of its formation, had strict control of labour recruiting, of course. Marconi killed the last of the fighting pirates, leaving only a few sneak-thieves, shot-in-the-back murderers and ship-seizers to flit briefly and with ignominy across the seafaring stage, mainly not in the Pacific.

A colourful period in at any rate the early story of Tasmania was the organised endeavour to bring out "respectable" women as brides for the woman-hungry locals. Such efforts never worked the way their organisers hoped they would, as many, many stories in the local newspapers show—particularly in the Hobart *Mercury*.

It seems to me that good material for a movie script is lurking in these. A piratical seizure of a "girl ship" really could be worked into a flamboyant musical!

Female Emigration to Australia
The Intention

The committee for promoting the EMIGRATION OF SINGLE WOMEN to AUSTRALIA, under whose management the Ships *Bussorah Merchant* and *Layton* were last year despatched with Female Emigrants, acting under the sanction of His Majesty's Secretary of State for the Colonies, hereby give Notice, that a fine Ship of about 500 tons burden, carrying an experienced surgeon, and a respectable person as superintendent to secure the comfort and protection of the Emigrants during the voyage, will sail from GRAVESEND, on Thursday, 1st of May next (beyond which day she will on no account be detained) direct for HOBART TOWN, VAN DIEMEN'S LAND. Single Women and Widows of good character, from 15 to 30 years of age, desirous of bettering their condition by emigrating to that healthy and highly prosperous Colony, where the number of Females compared with the entire population is greatly deficient, and where consequently from the great demand for servants, and other female employments, the wages are comparatively high, may obtain a passage on payment of Five Pounds only.

Those who are unable to raise that sum here will be allowed to give notes of hand payable in the Colony within a reasonable time after their arrival, when they have acquired the means to do so, as they will have the advantage of the Government grant in aid of their passage.

The Females who proceed by this conveyance will be taken care of on their first landing at Hobart Town; they will find there a list of the various situations to be obtained, and of the wages offered, and will be perfectly free to make their own selection; they will not be bound to any person, or subjected to any restraint, but will be, to all intents and purposes, perfectly free to act and decide for themselves.

Females in the country who may desire to avail themselves of the important advantages thus offered them, should apply by letter to "The Emigration Committee, London," under cover addressed to "The Under Secretary of State, Colonial Department, London." It will be necessary that the application be accompanied by a certificate of character from the Resident Minister of the parish, or from some other respectable persons to whom the applicant may be known; but the certificate of the Resident Minister is in all cases most desirable. Such females as may find it expedient may when approved by the Committee as fit persons to go by this conveyance be boarded temporarily in London, prior to embarkation, on payment of 7s per week.

All applications made under cover in the foregoing manner, or personally, will receive early answers, and all necessary information, by applying to

JOHN MARSHALL, Agents to the Committee,

26, Birchin-Lane, Cornhill,

Edward Forster, Chairman.

Note.—The Committee have the satisfaction to state that of 217 females who went out by the *Bussorah Merchant* 180 obtained good situations within three days of their landing, and the remainder were all well placed within a few days, under the advice of a Ladies' Committee formed in the Colony expressly to aid the females on their arrival.

The Performance

The present selection of female emigrants was made by a ladies' committee in London, one of the principal leaders of which committee was the celebrated Mrs Fry, well known to be both a praiseworthy and humane woman. Mrs Fry's practice has always been to keep the depraved and guilty separate from the innocent; and yet, in this present instance, the lady committee in question seems to have cared very little upon this point. . . . Could it be believed that any conscientious females of the saintly school would first entice respectable individuals to place themselves on board such a vessel as the *Princess Royal*, under the express understanding that only respectable individuals were to join them, and that then, in open defiance to all promises, that a lady committee should fill up the number required for the despatching of the vessel, from the Workhouse of St Giles, the Penitentiary, and the Magdalen, and other similar sinks of the Refuge for the Destitute? . . . Of the two hundred and odd females who have now arrived, about one fourth are really respectable. . . . The respectable part of the passengers cry out most grievously and with reason; they affirm that they were imposed upon; that promises upon promises were held out to them—that no female of suspicious character should be allowed to take her passage, otherwise they would never have left their respectable, though poverty-stricken homes. Mrs Fry and her coadjutants well know in what manner the lady committee kept those promises, when on the eve of the vessel's sailing, the outcasts of society, the dregs of the lowest quarters of the metropolis, were huddled on board, leaving a passage of five months to settle matters between the different classes.

Report in the Mercury, Hobart, Tasmania

The Woman Turns

Joseph Bowden, an absentee seaman from the *Strathfieldsaye*, was charged by Constable Stevens with disorderly conduct in the streets, and threatening to assault Miss Rudelhoff, one of the newly arrived actresses. It appeared that the defendant had been permitted to enjoy the conversation of the lady on board, and, therefore, made sure of a good reception on shore. The lady, however, thought fit to give him the cut direct, and an order to march at the same time, as she had some other friends with her. At this, Jack never having received an order of this kind before, and hearing the sound of the harmony within, winced a little, letting fly a volley of sea lingo, which the lady returned in her own style, until the storm raged high, which Jack threatened to end by giving little Dinah a broadside, when the Constable, attracted by the row, interfered, and removed him, slightly wounded, to the Bathurst Street cockpit. Reprimanded and discharged.

Report in the Mercury, Hobart

WINDJAMMER DAYS
The Real Thing

WINDJAMMER DAYS
The Real Thing

OFF at last I went to sea, under sail in the Merchant Service of course, my head full of Marryat, Bullen, *Peter the Whaler*, Drake, Cochrane, Dana, Jules Verne, Henty, and all the rest. Not all my reading or close acquaintance since childhood with big sailing-ships in port prepared me for the shock of the real sea, even in an old Tasman Sea barque. Here life was grim. The eternal four hours-on four-off of the sea watches gave little leisure to growing boys, and we were often called out for All Hands as well. Life was survival—never enough sleep, never enough to eat, too much menial work of scraping, scrubbing, polishing, crowded quarters, poor light, the wet seeping everywhere and the sea washing into our minute half-deck.

No, I didn't read much that first voyage, nor remember much I'd read before, except with scorn.

But we had a failed second mate with us, boss of the boys, a stern-faced young fellow aged about nineteen who had been sent back by the examiners at Sydney to serve another six months at sea after failing his examination for second mate. The failed second mate was determined not to fail again. He studied even during his short watch below: he studied all sorts of books to do with the profession of the sea.

Gradually the habit spread to us. In my second ship—another Pacific sailing barque—I brought along such classics as Reed's *Seamanship and Nautical Knowledge*, Nicholl's *Concise Guide*, Brown's *Signalling*. These were all I could afford.

For years I plugged away at this sort of stuff. We had

no tuition except from one another. At first I was a cadet in the old barque *Rothesay Bay,* but she soon sailed out of business. After that I shipped before the mast, as we all had to do. There were many officer-aspirants in the forecastles of those Pacific traders. We helped one another. One of our aims, doing all this, was to cut down the time we would have to spend expensively ashore, financing the essential minimum period at a school of navigation somewhere before going up for the B.O.T. second mate's certificate. What with time lost between ships, the general difficulty of staying in deep-sea sail during the early 1920s, and the very poor pay offered in the Finnish ships that some of us were forced to sail in, about all the time I looked like managing to finance ashore would be a couple of weeks.

So I read up on my *Reed's, Nicholl's, et al.,* with determination, and all the application I could bring to bear. They were simple books, direct and to the point. They were couched in the question and answer form. My copy of *Reed's,** the twentieth edition, kept strictly to facts through all its 640 pages.

It was indeed an alarming volume, but at first we did not need to learn it all. First came the second mate's examination, and we had to serve four years on deck in deep-water ships before we would be allowed to sit for that—four years, a good reference from each master with whom we sailed, a certificate of perfect vision (but not of health: that was taken for granted) and a determination to continue in an exacting, difficult and—then, at any rate—depression-beset profession.

But once started, I stuck with these books, passing also to Navigation. We had also the ships to teach us seamanship, no matter what Messrs Reed and Nicholl might have to say with their appalling questions and answers.

No fate was too dreadful for these pundits to deal with. Here, for instance, is a cheerful account of what to do when wrecked, as outlined in the ubiquitous *Reed's*:

* The excellent old text-book has only recently (1961) gone out of print. Friends at the Seafarers' Education Service tell me that seamen still frequently write in for it.

Q. If your vessel were driven among rocks, what means would you take to save the lives of all on board, and part or the whole of the cargo, if practicable?

A. If the rocks were near the shore or above water I would get the end of a good hawser made fast to the shore or to the highest rock within reach of the vessel, making the other end fast on board, and set it well tight with good purchase on which I could construct a traveller, with a chair or something of the same nature slung to it, and in this manner haul the passengers, crew, and property on shore.

Q. How would you get the end of the hawser made fast to the shore?

A. In all probability there would be people on the shore to make it fast. I would send it to them in the following manner:— By making a cork fender or some other buoyant substance fast to a small line (such as the log line or leadline), it would on being thrown overboard, drive on shore with a small line; a larger line might then be hauled to the shore and afterwards the hawser. If the place were uninhabited, other means might be used; I would endeavour to get on shore by swimming, with the assistance of a lifebuoy or in a boat or in any other manner which circumstances might suggest or permit; and as it is not probable that the vessel could be got off a bed of rocks, I would get what I could from her.

Q. Suppose the land inhabited, but the shore high and precipitous, so that no communication can be held between the foot and top of the cliff, how would you endeavour to open a communication with the people on the top?

A. It could not be done by floating a line ashore, nor by a man swimming; the line must be sent up into the air, this can be accomplished by means of a kite. Take a light hoop, but if you have none handy, take three light pieces of wood and bind them strongly together in the shape of a triangle, and cover it with canvas; attach three or four pieces of strong cord at equal distances to the wood, and fasten the ends securely to a light line. The shore being a lee shore the kite will be driven by the gale shorewards. If it reaches the top safely proceed as before described.

There used to be a kite patented by Captain Nares, R.N., with everything ready for instant use, and could be obtained in any port.

Q. If the vessel struck on a bed of sunken rocks, what would you do?

81

A. I would take to the boats, having them stowed with provisions and water in the best manner circumstances would permit. If the boats were disabled, I would construct a raft.

REED's *Seamanship and Nautical Knowledge*

THE USEFUL MR FINDLAY

In the charthouses of these sailing-ships (if they had no charthouse then in the master's quarters) was other required reading. In those days, voluminous and detailed accounts of ports and landfalls, dangers, sets, reefs, all that sort of thing (which now run to hundreds of expensive books in as many languages) were almost unknown. Cape Horners managed with half a dozen Findlays instead, and they did very well. Alex. Geo. Findlay, F.R.G.S., produced Directories for the Navigation of the Oceans—one for each ocean. They were enormous fat books running to a thousand pages or so, very useful for holding down deck logs or a navigation work-book in a gale of wind. Maybe they didn't go into too great detail—Findlay wrote for shipmasters who had time to stand off and on a place, if they were unsure of things—but the big fat tomes gave good sailing directions for the remotest spots on earth, and had time to offer the odd yarn about sundry places too.

I liked Findlay. For instance, he offered good advice on other matters besides navigation. Recommending a certain way of approaching the Burmese rice port of Akyab, he recounts the sad fact that one obstinate commander who did not follow the Findlay sailing track took fifty-nine days from the Straits of Malacca, causing his charterer to raise money at twenty per cent in order to finance the full cargo of rice he had undertaken to put on board, as the price of rice had risen steeply while he dallied.

Writing of the Crozet Isles (far from the track of any steamship today but on the route of big sailers running their Easting down) he recalls the story of the sealing cutter *Princess of Wales*, seventy-five tons, lost on Possession Island there on St Patrick's Day, 1821. The party lived on the flesh of sea elephants and "a plant resembling a cabbage, very bitter in taste but which, by boiling three or four hours, becomes palatable". One of the sealers was a Charles Med-yett Goodridge who, says Findlay, "wrote a narrative, the Robinson Crusoe style of which sufficed to keep him for some years by its sale in Devonshire and Cornwall".

It was good to know that, if one went up on Possession Island and managed to get ashore, all that was necessary was to boil the local cabbages for four hours or so daily, and then when rescued write a book about it for sale in the South-West of England.

The island of Comoro, in the Madagascar Channel, is recommended (though not properly surveyed and "very imperfectly represented on the charts") for engaging crews, for Findlay expressed a high opinion of the "fine race of men of remarkable stature" who inhabit the place.

I read of many, many islands and remote ports in the various Findlay volumes, and noted them all for subsequent visit if I ever had a "dream-ship" of my own.

I got to a lot of them, too.

JOHN MASEFIELD

At sea, we did not read only treatises on seamanship and navigation, and directories of the seven seas. We read everything we could lay hands on. This was in the days before the excellent Seafarers' Education Service in London supplied libraries and educational courses for mariners, but seamen's missions used to put books aboard, and friends would sometimes unload old volumes into Cape Horn or Tasman Sea forecastles. Everything was welcome, but nothing more so than books of the sea. They had to be written by *seamen*. The working seaman was a harsh critic of books dealing with his profession. Not for him the one-voyage chronicles (except Dana's; after all, Dana's voyage lasted two years) or the gush of self-professed and over-enthusiastic "lovers" of the sea and ships. He loved ships, too, but in his own way. As for the sea, how could that dispassionate and awful element be "loved" by anybody? He *fought* it—fought it with all he had, fought it to win, knowing well the costs of losing. As for love, that was for women, preferably young.

The real sea writers passed his tests—Conrad, Bone, Hendry (despite the fact that they were all masters), McFee (he, poor man, was an engineer, but that was forgiven), and John Masefield. There were some who remembered his *Wanderer*—a sea bitch if ever there was one, I heard a Welshman say once in the *Rothesay Bay*, who'd had a ship-mate drowned in her. But he liked Masefield. It was he who owned our only copy of his *Collected Poems*.

John Masefield has been Poet Laureate since 1930, which is a strange berth for a former Cape Horn sailing-ship apprentice. Some have fetched up in odder. Another such apprentice became Viceroy of India, and I have known of at least two others who became peers of the realm. At the usual early age of twelve or so, Masefield joined H.M.S. *Conway*, one of the old "wooden walls" of England which was then moored in the Mersey near Liverpool as a station-ary training-ship for the pre-sea training of boys wishing to become deck officers in the Merchant Service. The *Conway* was a stately three-decker of the classic type, and life aboard was tough.

It was probably even tougher in the big Liverpool four-poster *Wanderer,* to which the juvenile Masefield was bound apprentice, from the *Conway*, to serve his sea time. Though a big ship—she registered almost 3,000 tons and had a waterline of 309 feet—she was a skys'l-yarder and, indeed, looked something of a semi-clipper, despite the fact that she was not built until long after all the real clippers had gone out of business.

> All day they loitered by the resting ships
>   Telling their beauties over, taking stock:
> At night the verdict left my messmates' lips,
>   "The *Wanderer* is the finest ship in dock."
>
> I had not seen her, but a friend since drowned
>   Drew her, with painted ports, low, lovely, lean,
> Saying the "*Wanderer*, clipper, outward bound,
>   The loveliest ship my eyes have ever seen—"

So Poet Masefield wrote, years afterwards. Sailor Masefield knew better. That drowned friend might have been drowned from the *Wanderer*. Lovely as she was, she was what sailors call a *hoodoo* ship, killing or maiming somebody almost on every voyage, too often in trouble, no matter who might try to command her or how good her crew. She was a massive big ship, a carrier steel square-rigger, built with what sailors knew then as a "Liverpool house" filling her deck amidships, to break the force of the sea. (I saw some service in one of these Liverpool giants, another big sea-brute called *Bellands* which, as the *Forteviot*, was built by Potters—the *Wanderer*'s builders—in 1891. This *Forteviot* was distinguished for pulling tugs over, when they tried to hold her, and drowning men— she had pulled two tugs over once, in the Elbe—and her passages were all too frequently long, and bad. I was 151 days in her once, Melbourne to St Nazaire.)

The *Wanderer* had good lines and was well built and superbly strong, but I could more easily see Masefield as a sailor in some really perfect little barque such as Conrad's command the *Otago,* or the *J. T. North.* Masefield did not stay with her very long. He did not complete his sea time, leaving the *Wanderer* and taking up writing, which was a good thing for literature and the world in general.

As for the sea of sailing-ships, his long poem "Dauber" seemed to me to be not just his best picture of that life, but *the* best poem of that sort anywhere, by anybody. Here are extracts from it:

And all the air seemed full of gradual moan,
As though in those cloud-chasms the horns were blowing
The mort for gods cast out and overthrown,
Or for the eyeless sun plucked out and going.
Slow the low gradual moan came in the snowing;
The Dauber felt the prelude had begun,
The snowstorm fluttered by; he saw the sun

Show and pass by, gleam from one towering prison
Into another, vaster and more grim,
Which in dull crags of darkness had arisen
To muffle-to a final door on him.

The gods upon the dull crags lowered dim,
The pigeons chattered, quarrelling in the track.
In the south-west the dimness dulled to black.

Then came the cry of "Call all hands on deck!"
The Dauber knew its meaning; it was come:
Cape Horn, that tramples beauty into wreck,
And crumples steel and smites the strong man dumb.
Down clattered flying kites and staysails: some
Sang out in quick, high calls; the fairleads skirled,
And from the south-west came the end of the world.

"Caught in her ball-dress," said the Bosun, hauling;
"Lee-ay, lee-ay!" quick, high, came the men's call;
It was all wallop of sails and startled calling.
"Let fly!" "Let go!" "Clew up!" and "Let go all!"
"Now up and make them fast!" "Here, give us a haul!"
"Now up and stow them! Quick! By God! we're done!"
The blackness crunched all memory of the sun.

"Up!" said the Mate. "Mizen topgallants. Hurry!"
The Dauber ran, the others ran, the sails
Slatted and shook; out of the black a flurry
Whirled in fine lines, tattering the edge to trails.
Painting and art and England were old tales
Told in some other life to that pale man,
Who struggled with white fear and gulped and ran.

Fierce clamberers, some in oilskins, some in rags,
Hustling and hurrying up, up the steep stairs.
Before the windless sails were blown to flags,
And whirled like dirty birds athwart great airs,
Ten men in all, to get this mast of theirs
Snugged to the gale in time. "Up! Dam' you, run!"
The mizen topmast head was safely won.

"Lay out!" the Bosun yelled. The Dauber laid
Out on the yard, gripping the yard, and feeling
Sick at the mighty space of air displayed
Below his feet, where mewing birds were wheeling.
A giddy fear was on him; he was reeling.
He bit his lip half through, clutching the jack.
A cold sweat glued the shirt upon his back.

The yard was shaking, for a brace was loose.
He felt that he would fall; he clutched, he bent,
Clammy with natural terror to the shoes
While idiotic promptings came and went.
Snow fluttered on a wind-flaw and was spent;
He saw the water darken. Someone yelled.
"Frap it; don't stay to furl! Hold on!" He held.

Darkness came down—half darkness—in a whirl;
The sky went out, the waters disappeared.
He felt a shocking pressure of blowing hurl
The ship upon her side. The darkness speared
At her with wind; she staggered, she careered,
Then down she lay. The Dauber felt her go;
He saw his yard tilt downwards. Then the snow

Whirled all about—dense, multitudinous, cold—
Mixed with the wind's one devilish thrust and shriek,
Which whiffled out men's tears, deafened, took hold,
Flattening the flying drift against the cheek.
The yards buckled and bent, man could not speak.
The ship lay on her broadside; the wind's sound
Had devilish malice at having got her downed.

How long the gale had blown he could not tell,
Only the world had changed, his life had died.
A moment now was everlasting hell.
Nature an onslaught from the weather side,
A withering rush of death, a frost that cried,
Shrieked, till he withered at the heart; a hail
Plastered his oilskins with an icy mail.

"Cut!" yelled his mate. He looked—the sail was gone,
Blown into rags in the first furious squall;
The tatters drummed the devil's tattoo. On
The buckling yard a block thumped like a mall.
The ship lay—the sea smote her, the wind's bawl
Came, "loo, loo, loo!" The devil cried his hounds
On to the poor spent stag strayed in his bounds.

"Cut! Ease her!" yelled his mate; the Dauber heard.
His mate wormed up the tilted yard and slashed,
A rag of canvas skimmed like a darting bird.
The snow whirled, the ship bowed to it, the gear lashed,
The sea-tops were cut off and flung down smashed;
Tatters of shouts were flung, the rags of yells—
And clang, clang, clang, below beat the two bells.

"O God!" the Dauber moaned. A roaring rang,
Blasting the royals like a cannonade;
The backstays parted with a cracking clang,
The upper spars were snapped like twigs decayed—
Snapped at their heels, their jagged splinters splayed
Like white and ghastly hair erect with fear.
The Mate yelled, "Gone, by God, and pitched them clear!"

"Up!" yelled the Bosun; "up and clear the wreck!"
The Dauber followed where he led: below
He caught one giddy glimpsing of the deck
Filled with white water, as though heaped with snow.
He saw the streamers of the rigging blow
Straight out like pennons from the splintered mast,
Then, all sense dimmed, all was an icy blast.

Roaring from nether hell and filled with ice,
Roaring and crashing on the jerking stage,
An utter bridle given to utter vice,
Limitless power mad with endless rage
Withering the soul; a minute seemed an age.
He clutched and hacked at ropes, at rags of sail,
Thinking that comfort was a fairy-tale

Told long ago—long, long ago—long since
Heard of in other lives—imagined, dreamed—
There where the basest beggar was a prince
To him in torment where the tempest screamed,
Comfort and warmth and ease no longer seemed
Things that a man could know: soul, body, brain,
Knew nothing but the wind, the cold, the pain.

JOHN MASEFIELD: "Dauber"

Then there is the perfect picture of the Clipper loitering
South, on the Line, also in "Dauber":

Auckland Star

The four-masted barque *Pamir*, a German-built Cape Horner of the Hamburg Flying "P" line, here seen with a splendid quartering wind while sailing as a Second World War prize, under the New Zealand flag. Big midshipshouse was typical of the larger German sailing-ships. The *Pamir*, again sailing under the German flag, was blown over and foundered in a North Atlantic hurricane in 1957

The Portuguese naval school-ship *Sagres* is a former Cape Horner. Here she sails down the Tagus at Lisbon bound on an Atlantic cruise. Cross of the Order of Christ emblazons the sails as it did the sails of the Portuguese discoverers. Many nations use such ships for the indoctrination of their sea cadets. In 1962, the *Sagres* was replaced by a smaller barque

Above

Another sailing school-ship, the Norwegian full-rigger *Christian Radich* of Oslo, seen here getting under way from anchorage. The *Christian Radich* is one of three such training-ships in Norway, all privately financed. Japan, Italy, Spain, the U.S.S.R., the United States, Chile, Brazil, Indonesia, all maintain such ships, principally for their value in character training

Below

The pretty little barque *William Manson* (here painted by my artist friend Oswald Brett) would make an ideal British school-ship. Scots-built by Duthie in 1872, she carried China tea to Australia, became a coal hulk at Wellington, New Zealand, in 1914

Deep-loaded Cape Horners often rolled in heavy seas, which broke aboard. Such seas were dangerous as they easily knocked the sailors down, or swept them overboard. Lifelines are stretched along the deck for the men to cling to, but the sea could sweep them away from these. Work on deck was often more dangerous than work aloft

Above

For Arab seamen most of the work is on deck. Here aboard a Red Sea dhow the smiling *Nakhoda* (Master) and some of his turbanned crew are putting up an awning beside the primitive mast. We are bound from Aden towards the port of Gizan, in the Red Sea. Ropes are hand-made, sails are hand-sewn. We lived on fish from the sea, sailed the reef-littered coastal way only in the days, anchored by night

Below

Sailmakers aboard the famous *Herzogin Cecilie*: every sailor had to be able to use a palm and needle to repair sails. This is a Trade-wind sail being made ready to go aloft. I sailed in this fine four-master in 1928

To Mr. A. J. Villiers
with best wishes from
Charly "the Bosun".
formerly Boatswain of 4 mast Bark "Parma"
now with Count v. Luckner
M. Y. Mopelia January 1932.
New-York.

Sailing-ship boatswain of the old school, Charly Müller was with
Count Felix von Luckner of the *Seeadler,* rounded the Horn 37
times in a lifetime spent in square-rigged ships. Golden anchor
earrings are to "prevent" rheumatism. Charly was a bo's'n in the
South Pacific barques when I first went to sea, had already then
rounded the Horn 24 times under six flags. He never served in steam

Fox Photos

Tramp steamship on Channel rocks from which she will never come
off. Her bottom is pierced and even on a quiet day the seas
break right over her. No ship could stand much of this. Many
sailing-ships ended the same way, several in the same spot off the
stormy coast of rock-bound Cornwall. Vessel is typical smaller
tramp. Crew have escaped by their boats: the davits swing empty

Fox Photos

Long, tall, lean, magnificent, the Cunarder *Queen Mary* lies alongside at Southampton preparing for yet another voyage to New York. She and her consort *Queen Elizabeth* are the largest, grandest pair of regular Transatlantic "ferries" ever built. Winged-out bridge towers above dock-side cranes. From lookout post similar to that on the *Queen Mary's* foremast, *Titanic's* lookout first saw the ice which sank her

Out of the air a time of quiet came,
Calm fell upon the heaven like a drouth;
The brass sky watched the brassy water flame.
Drowsed as a snail the clipper loitered south
Slowly, with no white bone across her mouth;
No rushing glory, like a queen made bold,
The Dauber strove to draw her as she rolled.

There the four leaning spires of canvas rose,
Royals and skysails lifting, gently lifting,
White like the brightness that a great fish blows
When billows are at peace and ships are drifting;
With mighty jerks that set the shadows shifting,
The courses tugged their tethers: a blue haze
Drifted like ghosts of flocks come down to graze.

There the great skyline made her perfect round,
Notched now and then by the sea's deeper blue;
A smoke-smutch marked a steamer homeward bound,
The haze wrought all things to intenser hue.
In tingling impotence the Dauber drew
As all men draw, keen to the shaken soul
To give a hint that might suggest the whole.

THE EMIGRANT SHIPS

I saw enough of the emigrant ships to know what Masefield
—a sailing-ship sailor himself—was talking about in this:

Those splendid ships, each with her grace, her glory,
Her memory of old song or comrade's story,
Still in my mind the image of life's need,
Beauty in hardest action, beauty indeed.
"They built great ships and sailed them" sounds most brave,
Whatever arts we have or fail to have;
I touch my country's mind, I come to grips
With half her purpose thinking of these ships.

That art untouched by softness, all that line
Drawn ringing hard to stand the test of brine;
That nobleness and grandeur, all that beauty

89

Born of a manly life and bitter duty;
That splendour of fine bows which yet could stand
The shock of rollers never checked by land.
That art of masts, sail-crowded, fit to break,
Yet stayed to strength, and back-stayed into rake,
The life demanded by that art, the keen
Eye-puckered, hard-case seamen, silent, lean,
They are grander things than all the art of towns,
Their tests are tempests, and the sea that drowns.
They are my country's line, her great art done
By strong brains labouring on the thought unwon;
They mark our passage as a race of men,
Earth will not see such ships as those agen.

JOHN MASEFIELD

STORIES OF THE SAILING SEA, ABLY CHRONICLED

The later-day sailing Merchant Service was most fortunate in its chroniclers—few (you can count the real ones on the fingers of one hand), but magnificent! Conrad, Masefield, Bone, Shalimar (Captain F. C. Hendry)—there you have them. And all professional seamen too—*seamen* first, writers afterwards. I think there is a reason for this. At sea, serving his ships, the seaman had time to think but not to write. He had to think through things. His duties, if he carried them out properly, insisted upon integrity of character. The nature of his watchkeeping caused him to be a reflective person. He had need to think things through, and the ship gave him time—usually. He had need also to make decisions, rapidly, and they must be the *right* decisions, instantly made and most clearly conveyed in minimal and incisive prose. Of what better stuff could books be made?

All these writers are sailing-ship seamen of long experience, all save Masefield, masters. They did not only know their subject through and through: they *lived* it. Conrad, Sir David Bone, Captain Hendry—all were master mariners, trained in sail. Masefield began as a sailing-ship apprentice, professionally bound to the sea.

Such men did not rush into print with one-voyage books. They got to know their subject first and had something of value to offer.

Read a little Conrad again, for instance, about his *Narcissus* flung by the sea over on her side—her "beam ends", seamen say.

Touch and Go

The sky low by the horizon took on the delicate tints of pink and yellow like the inside of a rare shell. And higher, where it glowed with a pearly sheen, a small black cloud appeared, like a forgotten fragment of the night set in a border of dazzling gold. The beams of light skipped on the crests of waves. The eyes of men turned to the eastward. The sunlight flooded their weary faces. They were giving themselves up to fatigue as though they had done for ever with their work. On Singleton's black oilskin coat the dried salt glistened like hoarfrost. He hung on by the wheel, with open and lifeless eyes. Captain Allistoun, unblinking, faced the rising sun. His lips stirred, opened for the first time in twenty-four hours, and with a fresh firm voice, he cried, "Wear ship!"

The commanding sharp tones made all these torpid men start like a sudden flick of a whip. Then again, motionless where they lay, the force of habit made some of them repeat the order in hardly audible murmurs. Captain Allistoun glanced down at his crew, and several, with fumbling fingers and hopeless movements, tried to cast themselves adrift. He repeated impatiently, "Wear ship. Now then, Mr Baker, get the men along. What's the matter with them?"—"Wear ship. Do you hear there?— Wear ship!" thundered out the boatswain suddenly. His voice seemed to break through a deadly spell. Men began to stir and crawl. "I want the foretopmast staysail run up smartly," said the master, very loudly; "if you can't manage it standing up you must do it lying down—that's all. Bear a hand!"—"Come along! Let's give the old girl a chance," urged the boatswain.—"Aye, aye! Wear ship!" exclaimed quavering voices. The forecastle men, with reluctant faces, prepared to go forward. Mr Baker pushed ahead, grunting, on all fours to show the way, and they followed him over the break. The others lay still with a vile hope in their hearts of not being required to move till they got saved or drowned in peace.

After some time they could be seen forward appearing on the

forecastle head, one by one in unsafe attitudes; hanging on to the rails, clambering over the anchors; embracing the crosshead of the windlass or hugging the forecapstan. They were restless with strange exertions, waved their arms, knelt, lay flat down, staggered up, seemed to strive their hardest to go overboard. Suddenly a small white piece of canvas fluttered amongst them, grew larger, beating. Its narrow head rose in jerks—and at last it stood distended and triangular in the sunshine. "They have done it!" cried the voices aft. Captain Allistoun let go the rope he had round his wrist and rolled to leeward headlong. He could be seen casting the lee main braces off the pins while the backwash of waves splashed over him. "Square the main yard!" he shouted up to us—who stared at him in wonder. We hesitated to stir. "The main brace, men. Haul! haul anyhow! Lay on your backs and haul!" he screeched, half-drowned down there. We did not believe we could move the main yard, but the strongest and the less discouraged tried to execute the order. Others assisted half-heartedly. Singleton's eyes blazed suddenly as he took a fresh grip of the spokes. Captain Allistoun fought his way up to windward. "Haul, men! Try to move it! Haul, and help the ship." His hard face worked suffused and furious. "Is she going off, Singleton?" he cried—"Not a move yet, sir," croaked the old seaman in a horribly hoarse voice—"Watch the helm, Singleton," spluttered the master, "Haul, men! Have you no more strength than rats? Haul, and earn your salt." Mr Creighton, on his back, with a swollen leg and a face as white as a piece of paper, blinked his eyes; his bluish lips twitched. In the wild scramble men grabbed at him, crawled over his hurt leg, knelt on his chest. He kept perfectly still, setting his teeth without a moan, without a sigh. The master's ardour, the cries of that silent man, inspired us. We hauled and hung in bunches on the rope. We heard him say with violence to Donkin, who sprawled abjectly on his stomach, "I will brain you with this belaying pin if you don't catch hold of the brace," and that victim of men's injustice, cowardly and cheeky, whimpered: "Are you goin' to murder us now?" while with sudden desperation he gripped the rope. Men sighed, shouted, hissed meaningless words, groaned. The yards moved, came slowly square against the wind, that hummed loudly on the yardarms—"Going off, sir," shouted Singleton, "she's just started."—"Catch a turn with that brace. Catch a turn!" clamoured the master. Mr Creighton, nearly suffocated and unable to move, made a mighty effort, and with his left hand managed to nip the rope. "All fast!" cried someone. He closed his eyes as if going off into a swoon, while huddled together about the brace we watched with scared looks what the ship would do now.

She went off slowly as though she had been weary and disheartened like the men she carried. She paid off very gradually, making us hold our breath till we choked, and as soon as she had brought the wind abaft the beam she started to move, and fluttered our hearts. It was awful to see her, nearly overturned, begin to gather way and drag her submerged side through the water. The deadeyes of the rigging churned the breaking seas. The lower half of the deck was full of mad whirlpools and eddies; and the long line of the lee rail could be seen showing black now and then in the swirls of a field of foam as dazzling and white as a field of snow. The wind sang shrilly amongst the spars; and at every slight lurch we expected her to slip to the bottom sideways from under our backs. When dead before it she made the first distinct attempt to stand up, and we encouraged her with a feeble and discordant howl. A great sea came running up aft and hung for a moment over us with a curling top; then crashed down under the counter and spread out on both sides into a great sheet of bursting froth. Above its fierce hiss we heard Singleton's croak: "She is steering!" He had both his feet now planted firmly on the grating, and the wheel spun fast as he eased the helm. "Bring the wind on the port quarter and steady her!" called out the master, staggering to his feet, the first man up from amongst our prostrate heap. One or two screamed with excitement: "She rises!" Far away forward, Mr Baker and three others were seen erect and black on the clear sky, lifting their arms, and with open mouths as though they had been shouting all together. The ship trembled, trying to lift her side, lurched back, seemed to give up with a nerveless dip, and suddenly with an unexpected jerk swung violently to windward, as though she had torn herself out from a deadly grasp. The whole immense volume of water, lifted by her deck, was thrown bodily across to starboard. Loud cracks were heard. Iron ports breaking open thundered with ringing blows. The water topped over the starboard rail with the rush of a river falling over a dam. The sea on deck, and the seas on every side of her, mingled together in a deafening roar. She rolled violently. We got up and were helplessly run or flung about from side to side. Men, rolling over and over, yelled, "The house will go!"—"She clears herself!" Lifted by a towering sea she ran along with it for a moment, spouting thick streams of water through every opening of her wounded sides. The lee braces having been carried away or washed off the pins, all the ponderous yards on the fore swung

93

from side to side and with appalling rapidity at every roll. The men forward were seen crouching here and there with fearful glances upwards at the enormous spars that whirled about over their heads. The torn canvas and the end of broken gear streamed in the wind like wisps of hair. Through the clear sunshine, over the flashing turmoil and uproar of the seas, the ship ran blindly, dishevelled and headlong, as if fleeing for her life; and on the poop we spun, we tottered about, distracted and noisy. We all spoke at once in a thin babble; we had the aspect of invalids and the gestures of maniacs. Eyes shone, large and haggard, in smiling, meagre faces that seemed to have been dusted over with powdered chalk. We stamped, clapped our hands, feeling ready to jump and do anything; but in reality hardly able to keep on our feet. Captain Allistoun, hard and slim, gesticulating madly from the poop at Mr Baker: "Steady these foreyards! Steady them the best you can!" On the main deck, men excited by his cries splashed, dashing aimlessly here and there with the foam swirling up to their waists. Apart, far aft, and alone by the helm, old Singleton had deliberately tucked his white beard under the top button of his glistening coat. Swaying upon the din and tumult of the seas, with the whole battered length of the ship launched forward in a rolling rush before his steady old eyes, he stood rigidly still, forgotten by all, and with an attentive face. In front of his erect figure only the two arms moved crosswise with a swift and sudden readiness, to check or urge again the rapid stir of circling spokes. He steered with care.

JOSEPH CONRAD: *The Nigger of the "Narcissus"*

ANOTHER CASE

Captain James S. Learmont, formerly Superintendent of Pilots at Harwich, is another kind of seaman-writer, a one-book man, who distils a lifetime of professional experience into the one rather bald account. Bald it may be, but the facts are there. Learmont was an outstanding sailing-ship captain in the last days of sail, when such were becoming increasingly rare (why stay in the doomed long-voyage sailing-ships when obviously one's professional future should be in steam?). He was not always popular among his brother master-mariners, for he was given to exposing rackets in which some of them found profit at the expense of their owners and their ships. He did not subscribe to die-hard doctrines, nor believe that only ancient grey-beards (seamen aged thirty and over) were fit to be officers in Cape Horn ships. For several years, when older officers proved unsatisfactory, Learmont sailed a big steel ship with two *boys* as his mates, both well under twenty: but he had trained those boys, and brought them up properly.

On another occasion, finding a mean racket in a certain well-known port on the west coast of South America whereby many ships had been lost, and some masters had profited, Learmont exposed the chicanery forthwith and would have no part in it. Ships, he found, were in the habit of accepting considerably less ballast than they were charged with, slippery agents and conniving masters sharing the criminal difference, while the ship went to sea in peril. Learmont made a noise. It was not popular to make a noise, for the echoes might reach the owners. Learmont had other standards of popularity.

Learmont writes as a man sure of himself. He knows his business as a sailing-ship master thoroughly, and he *knows* he knows it. He is never bothered with doubts. He feels himself not only a master in sail, properly qualified, but master of any situation likely to arise aboard a deep-sea sailing-ship, ever.

This impression runs through the only book he wrote, and some of his fellow seamen did not care for it. I think his view of his own capacity is a fair one. He was one of those rare men who, having taken the trouble to gain thorough mastery of their chosen profession and fortified by years of successful practice of that mastery, survey the vast horde of the mediocre who had never gained much (or perhaps any) knowledge of anything, with unfeigned indifference. What the mediocre thought of him he just did not care—as neither did, for example, Field-Marshal Lord Montgomery. It never occurred to Learmont to consider their views.

He writes as if he had full knowledge of his stuff. He had. Most other masters would almost certainly have lost the *Bengairn* that voyage.

Here he is, with his ship thrown over on her beam ends in a gale.

This continual loss of ships on passage from Newcastle to the West Coast had naturally given me concern for a long time, as I knew it formed a large part of the work of a sailing-ship. When I had loaded at Newcastle with the *Brenda* in 1906, I didn't worry as the cargo was the light gas coal and it was only with difficulty that we got the total weight under hatches. That cargo couldn't shift, if it filled the ship. I had talked to my father for years about these losses and he considered that the cause was the cargo shifting. In cases of fire there was always the chance of being picked up, for as a rule you had time to abandon ship, whereas in these cases no one was ever saved. I always ended the discussion by saying that if ever my cargo shifted I would chop the masts out of her.

I had decided to sail early in the day as I did not consider it desirable to leave with darkness coming on, and a new crew. The pilot and tugs were ordered for 8 a.m., but all day we lay at the buoy waiting, until just before dark the old tug *Bungaree* came alongside by herself to tow us out to sea. On account of her age, she was not certified beyond the limits of Newcastle harbour. In reply to my demand for the reason of delay and the whereabouts of the second tug he told me that the *Champion* was short of a cook and so could not go to sea. As soon as we neared the Nobbies the tug signalled his intention of casting off the towrope; as the wind was fair I did not mind.

With three lower topsails set and the foresail, the *Bengairn* was speeding away towards the southeast before a rapidly increasing wind. My barometer was low, the sea was one mass of phosphorescence and it somehow seemed uncanny. I cannot explain my change of attitude on this particular occasion in relation to the weather; it was most unusual for me to be under only lower topsails and steering a course. There was of course the factor of a new crew, less than thirty-six hours on board, and the consideration that we were entering a part of the ocean where you commonly ran, as we did, right into bad weather after leaving port. She was going away before the northerly gale doing eight or nine knots, so there was not much loss in time, yet somehow I had a premonition that I should be cautious.

We had had a great number of rats in the *Bengairn*, but whilst we were in Newcastle my wife noted that they were not about as usual and openly said she didn't like it. Her fears were strengthened as somehow it got aft that Frank had noticed the rats leaving the ship in hordes one night. I naturally pooh-poohed the whole thing as nonsense, saying that the last of the loose grain from our previous cargo had been eaten by them, and that they were leaving to look for food.

Next day it blew much harder and the seas were rising, but she went along without doing any damage. On the following day the seas were very heavy and, with the wind on the quarter, she was lurching heavily. After one particularly heavy lurch I heard an ominous sound coming from the hold and she failed to right herself. The Jap was at the wheel. I ordered him to put the helm up so that we would get away before the wind and so bring wind and sea astern, but she was as if dead and failed to answer the helm. First I ordered them to let fly the lower mizzen topsail sheets in an endeavour to make her pay off, then the lower main topsail sheets, but the list increased. The sea was now making a clean breach of the whole of her starboard side. To relieve her, I next ordered the fore sheet to be let go, and Frank literally dived under water to do this; how he managed to keep himself from being caught in the wire foresheet, that was torn out by the threshing of the foresail after he had slacked it off, I don't know.

On deck the scene was one of desolation; as the big combers came along they swept everything before them overboard. From the minute she heeled over it was really a terrifying sight, a fine ship on her beam ends with the seas battering the whole of her starboard side as she lay helpless, unable to escape from their fury as they stripped her of anything that was movable.

The ship was to all intents and purposes in her death throes, but we had to save her if possible in order to save ourselves. All the boats on the lee side had been swept away, and with the heavy list you could have walked outboard on her weather side, so it was useless to think of trying to lower the one remaining lifeboat. There was a movement by some of the crew while I was down in the hold to lower this boat, but Frank stopped it saying, "When the Capen says lower that boat, we'll lower it, but not before. Get away from here." As he was carrying an axe his words had weight.

The heel of the ship was such that one-half of No. 2 hatch between the main and mizzen masts was under water, and this hatch now became our principal concern as the tarpaulins started to wash off. Unknown to us, the bulwark stanchions under the strain of the ship lying on her side had been sheared off in the

97

scuppers and water was pouring in there as well as through the No. 2 hatch. When the carpenter sounded the well he found four feet six inches of water. As the sounding pipe was amidships, she must have had much more on the lee side.

Close the hatch we must if we wanted to see daylight again. Every conceivable plan was tried to get spare tarpaulins over it with lashings but they were washed back on us. I then decided on trying with a brand new lower topsail bent on to a new rope as if it were the jackstay on a yard. After getting sufficient rope on each end we hove it tight by using the two capstans on the weather side which was free of water. When the sail was bent we furled it, using rope yarns as stops. Easing the capstans, on our hands and knees we pushed the furled sail over the combings, literally diving as the sea was breaking clean over us, but it soaked the sail and somehow helped by increasing its weight. At last with a final heave over it went, and we yelled, "Heave away!" The rope, a four-inch manila, took the strain; the sea couldn't budge him. Then by diving again we cut the stops and the sea helping us, covered the breach with the sail. With an additional coil of rope we were able to secure it firmly around the hatch coamings.

We had secured the hatch but our position was still perilous. With so much water in the ship, her freeboard under ordinary conditions would be reduced by two feet; but now, on her beam ends, it was only a matter of time how long she would last.

With darkness coming on and the gale unabated I decided to cut the topmast backstays and let the top hamper go. As soon as the seizings were cut on the mizzen the topmasts doubled over above the cap and the whole lot went in a mighty crash. Frank was like a Trojan as he wielded saw and axe, encouraging his helpers in forcible language.

The loss of the top hamper on the mizzen relieved the ship considerably so I decided to cut the main away as well. This action eased the leverage for in all on each mast, topmast and topsail yards, topgallant yards and masts with royal yards would weigh about forty tons. Eighty tons was not much, you might say, but at an angle of nearly 60° of heel, it was only when the ship was relieved of this weight that you realized how much it had affected her. Though the lee rail was submerged the force of the seas breaking on the hatch was not so heavy and I could see we had still a fighting chance. On soundings being taken we found that the securing of the hatch had been successful as the water had not increased. Those who understood the boiler were put on the job of making preparation for raising steam to pump the ship out. Mustering all hands on the poop I fed them with what food we could get, which, as the galley was washed out, was bottled stout and Australian biscuits.

I didn't see my wife for two days although I had news about her and the two children from the apprentices. As our quarters had been completely gutted she managed somehow with the help of the apprentices to get herself and the children up into the charthouse.

By way of the sail-locker, all hands got into the after hold and started to move the coal over from starboard to port by means of a basket and trolley. On account of the heavy list the incline was such that a tackle was necessary to pull the trolley up to windward. I found that it was possible to walk along the stringer plate the whole length of the port side, for all the 'tween deck cargo had gone over against the shifting boards. On the starboard side I could walk along amidships by using the beams alongside of the shifting boards; there the 'tween deck cargo had gone bodily against the ship's side.

Meanwhile, the men working on the donkey boiler had filled the boiler with water, and started to raise steam. It was, in the circumstances, a very trying operation as everything had to be fitted under great difficulty. Even the shipping of the funnel was a problem. When we did get steam we were very scared about the effect of the list on the boiler. The gauge glass was on the starboard side of the boiler so you could not depend on it, and the danger of leaving the furnace crown exposed on the weather side was great. However, we got the pumps going by using the winch and a messenger chain.

Night and day the trimming went on with only brief stops for food and drink. Once I felt that we were reasonably safe, with the improvement in the weather, I decided that the crew would do better if they had rest. I was afraid of going to sleep myself, so I called for a volunteer to stand with me while the rest had a sleep. Without any hesitation a coloured man, Jeremiah Wilson, stepped forward, and he stood with me. Frank had been a tower of strength through it all, but now he was dead beat.

After the men had had a rest, by the aid of hand pumping we were able to reduce the soundings in the well while giving the donkey boiler a rest. Owing to the list we could only use the weather pump handle so to aid it a "bull rope" was used which any number of hands could tally on to.

With the ship gradually righting herself through pumping and trimming we were faced with a new danger; the broken spars that were hanging over were cutting the lower rigging at every movement and I was afraid that if they sagged further the jagged steel might pierce her under water, which would finish us, so I decided to get clear of them somehow. With the mate I went aloft, which was more a case of crawling than climbing on account of the list. On the lower cap we were over the sea and just at this critical moment my wife came on deck, the first time that she had been able to get out. With an axe I cut the wire brace runner that was holding the wreckage and as soon as I got it halfway through the whole lot went. My wife told me that it was very wrong for us two who were so important for the safety of the ship to go on such a dangerous job. She was right, but one doesn't see danger in such circumstances.

Working night and day at trimming the cargo and at the pumps we were gaining ground. I was at both jobs along with the crew, hungry, dirty and sleepy. The passing of days had not meant anything to me but about now I realized that it was five days since the cargo shifted.

Although the wreckage was now clear of the ship, it was, on account of the lee backstays, still attached, but at least eighty feet under water. By means of life-lines we were now able to get down to slip the screws and let it go. By this time we had secured the yards on the foremast and set some sails. At last she was answering to her helm. As Sydney was our nearest port we set course for there.

JAMES LEARMONT: *Master in Sail*

CAPTAIN SIR DAVID BONE

Captain Sir David W. Bone, K.B., C.B.E., Doctor of Laws of the University of Glasgow, former Commodore-Master of the Anchor Line in the Transatlantic and Eastern trades, and writer of half a dozen excellent books on the sea, was a member of a talented Scots family which includes also artists, journalists, and outstanding men of letters. Born at Glasgow in 1874, he went to sea in the classic manner as an apprentice in a deep-sea sailing-ship, when he was sixteen. His ship was the *City of Florence*, a graceful full-rigger well known upon the Cape Horn road. Like many another adventurous young seaman, he stayed in sail after completing his four years' indentures, and was second mate under the well-known "Bully" Martin in the ship *Loch Ness*. Captain Martin was a hard man to serve and a harder to please, and the *Loch Ness* was run on rugged lines, but her second mate left her with an excellent reference. "Mr Bone was a good seaman, able and alert," wrote the Bully; and that curt and well-earned line was worth more than a book of praise from most other men.

Like many another adventurous young seaman, too, Bone soon found that he had to go in steam as a career, if he was going to get anywhere. He joined the Scots Anchor Line in 1899, and rose there to be Commodore. Though then dedicated to the service of powered vessels, his sea life continued to be adventurous. He served at sea throughout both World Wars. He commanded famous Atlantic passenger liners. He was ten years in one ship—as second officer, chief officer, and finally master—on the Scotland–India run. His passengers included Captain Conrad (going to America for his first visit) and his crew once numbered another famed seaman-writer, William McFee, who signed articles in the R.M.S. *Tuscania* under Bone as "Master's Clerk". His duties there included charge of a Bone innovation aboard, the High Seas Book Shop.

Sir David's father was a journalist in Glasgow, and the son took naturally to the pen. In his biographical *Landfall at Sunset,* he remarks that the poor pay of Merchant Service officers of those days may have had something to do with his urge to write. Whatever the reason, he wrote splendidly, and his *Brassbounder* is the classic account of an apprentice's life in the last days of sail. He wrote other books—*Merchant-men-at-Arms, The Lookoutman, Broken Stowage, Capstan Bars,* among them, all successful on both sides of the Atlantic.

Here is a selection from *The Brassbounder,* based on the author-seaman's experiences in the *City of Florence,* in the Californian trade. *The Brassbounder* was published in 1910, and I well remember my delight when I first read it. (It helped me to decide on a career in sail, too.) Since then, the number of such books has turned to legion and many of them are good. Captain Bone's was the first. It remains the best.

"T' Wind'ard!"

For over a week of strong westerly gales we had kept the open sea, steering to the north as best the wind allowed. A lull had come—a break in the furious succession, though still the sea ran high—and the Old Man, in part satisfied that he had made his northing, put the helm up and squared away for the land. In this he was largely prompted by the coasting pilot (sick of a long unprofitable passage—on a "lump sum" basis), who confidently asked to be shown but one speck of Irish land, and, "I'll tell 'oo the road t' Dub-lin, Capt'in!"

Moderately clear at first, but thickening later, as we closed the land, it was not the weather for running in on a dangerous coast, ill-lighted and unmarked, but, had we waited for clear weather, we might have marked time to the westward until the roses came; the wind was fair, we were over-long on our voyage; sheet and brace and wind in squared sail thrummed a homeward song for us as we came in from the west.

At close of a day of keen sailing, the outposts of the Irish coast, bleak, barren, inhospitable, lay under our lee—a few bold rocks, around and above wreathed in sea-mist, and the never-dying Atlantic swell breaking heavily at base.

"Iss, indeed, Capt'in! The Stags! The Stags of Broad-haven I tell 'oo," said the pilot, scanning through his glasses with an easy assurance. "Indeed to goodness, it iss the best landfall I haf ever seen, Capt'in!"

Though pleased with his navigation, the Old Man kept his head. "Aye, aye," he said. "The Stags, eh? Well, we'll haul up t' th' wind anyway—t' make sure!" He gave the order, and went below to his charts.

Rolling heavily, broad to the sea and swell, we lay awhile. There was no sign of the weather clearing, no life in the grey mist that hung dense over the rugged coast-line. On deck again, the Old Man stared long and earnestly at the rocky islets, seeking a further guidemark. In the waning daylight they were fast losing shape and colour. Only the breaking sea, white and sightly, marked them bold in the grey mist-laden breath of the Atlantic. "Present themselves, consisting of four high rocky islets of from two thirty-three to three ought-six feet in height, an' steep-to" he said, reading from a book of sailing directions. "Damme! I can only see three." To the pilot, "D'ye know the Stags well, Mister? Are ye sure of ye're ground?"

"*Wel, wel!* Indeed, Capt'in" (Mr Williams laughed). "I know the Stags, yess! Ass well ass I know Carnarvon! The Stags of Broad-haven, I tell 'oo. When I wass master of the *Ann Pritchard,* of Beaumaris, it wass always to the West of Ireland we would be goin'. Summer and winter, three years, I tell 'oo, before I came to pilotin', an' there iss not many places between the Hull and Missen Head that I haf nor seen in daylight an' dark. It iss the Stags, indeed! East, south-east now, Capt'in, an' a fine run to Sligo Bar!"

Still unassured, the Old Man turned his glasses on the rocky group. "One—two—three—perhaps that was the fourth just open to the south"—and they certainly tallied with the description in the book—"high, steep-to." A cast of the lead brought no decision. Forty-seven! He might be ten miles north and south by that and former soundings. It was rapidly growing dark, the wind freshening. If he did not set course by the rocks—Stags they seemed to be—he would lose all benefit of landfall—would spend another week or more to the west-ward waiting for a rare slant on this coast of mist and foul weather! Already eighteen days from Falmouth! The chance of running in was tempting! Hesitating, uncertain, he took a step or two up and down the poop, halting at turns to stare anxiously at the rocks, in the wind's eye, at the great Atlantic combers welling up and lifting the barque to leeward at every rise. On the skylight sat Mr Williams, smiling and clucking in his beard that "he did not know the Stags, indeed!"

"We haul off, Pilot," said stout Old Jock, coming at a decision. "If it had been daylight . . . perhaps . . . but I'm for takin' no risks. They may be th' Stags, belike they are, but I'm no' goin' oan in weather like this! We'll stand out t' th' norrard—'mainyards forward, Mister'—till daylight onyway!"

Sulkily we hauled the yards forward and trimmed sail, leaving the rocks to fade under curtain of advancing night, our high hopes of making port dismissed. The "navigators" among us were loud of their growling, as the ship lurched and wallowed in the trough of the sea, the decks waist-high with a wash of icy water—a change from the steadiness and comfort of a running ship.

Night fell black dark. The moon not risen to set a boundary to sea and sky; no play of high light on the waste of heaving water; naught but the long inky ridges, rolling out of the west, that, lifting giddily to crest, sent us reeling into the windless trough. On the poop the Old Man and Pilot tramped fore and aft, talking together of landfalls and coasting affairs. As they came and went, snatches of their talk were borne to us, the watch on deck—

sheltering from the weather at the break. The Old Man's "Aye, ayes," and "Goad, man's," and the voluble Welshman's "Iss, indeed, Capt'in," and "I tell 'oo's." The Pilot was laying off a former course of action. " ' . . . Mister Williams,' he said, 'I can see that 'oo knows th' coast,' he said, 'an' . . . I 'oodn't go in myself,' he said; 'but if 'oo are sure—' "

"*Brea-kers a-head!*"—a stunning period to his tale, came in a long shout, a scream almost, from the look-out!

Both sprang to the lee rigging, handing their eyes to shield the wind and spray. Faint as yet against the sombre monotone of sea and sky, a long line of breaking water leapt to their gaze, then vanished, as the staggering barque drove to the trough; again—again; there could be no doubt. Breakers! On a lee shore! !

"*Mawdredd an'll* O Christ! The Stags, Capt'in. . . . My God!" Wholly unmanned, muttering in Welsh and English, Mr Williams ran to the compass to take bearings.

Old Jock came out of the rigging. Then, in a steady voice, more ominous than a string of oaths, "Luff! Down helm m'lad, an' keep her close!" And to the Pilot, "Well? What d'ye make of it, Mister?"

"Stags, Capt'in! *Diwedd i!* That I should be mistake . . . The others . . . God knows! . . . If it iss the Stags, Capt'in . . . the passage t' th' south'ard . . . I know it . . . we can run . . . if it iss the Stags, Capt'in!"

"An' if it's no' th' Stags! M' Goad! Hoo many Stags d'ye know, Mister? No! No! We'll keep th' sea, if she can weather thae rocks . . . and if she canna!" A mute gesture—then passionately, "T'hell wi' you an' yer b——y Stags: I back ma ship against a worthless pilot! All hands, there, Mister—mains'l an' to'galn's'l oan her! Up, ye hounds; up, if ye look fur dry berryin'!"

All hands! No need for a call! "Breakers ahead"—the words that sent us racing to the yards, to out knife and whip at the gaskets that held our saving power in leash. Quickly done, the great mainsail blew out, thrashing furiously till steadied by tack and sheet. Then topgal'n'sail, the spars buckling to overstrain; staysail, spanker—never was canvas crowded on a ship at such a pace; a mighty fear at our hearts that only frenzied action could allay.

Shuddering, she lay down to it, the lee rail entirely awash, the decks canted at a fearsome angle; then righted—a swift, vicious lurch, and her head sweeping wildly to windward till checked by the heaving helmsman. The wind that we had thought moderate when running before it now held at half a gale. To that she might have stood weatherly, but the great western swell—spawn of uncounted gales—was matched against her, rolling up to check the windward snatches and sending her reeling to leeward in a smother of foam and broken water.

A gallant fight! At the weather gangway stood Old Jock, legs apart and sturdy, talking to his ship.

"Stand, good spars," he would say, casting longing eyes aloft. Or, patting the taffrail with his great sailor hands, "Up tae it, ye bitch! Up!! Up!!" as, raising her head, streaming in cascade from a sail-pressed plunge, she turned to meet the next great wall of water that set against her. "She'll stand it, Mister," to the Mate at his side. "She'll stand it, an' the head gear holds. If she starts that!"—he turned his palms out—"If she starts th' head gear, Mister!"

"They'll hold, Sir! . . . good gear," answered the Mate, hugging himself at thought of the new landyards, the stout Europe gammon lashings, he had rove off when the boom was rigged. Now was the time when Sanny Armstrong's spars would be put to the test. The relic of the ill-fated *Glenisla* now a shapely to'gallant mast, was bending like a whip! "Good iron," he shouted as the backstays twanged a high note of utmost stress.

Struggling across the heaving deck, the Pilot joined the group. Brokenly, shouting down the wind, "She'll never do it, Capt'in, I tell 'oo! . . . An' th' tide. . . . Try th' south passage . . . Stags, sure! . . . See them fair now! . . . Th' south passage, Capt'in. . . . It iss some years, indeed, but . . . I know. *Diwedd an'l!* She'll never weather it, Capt'in!"

"Aye . . . and weather it . . . an' the gear holds! Goad, man! Are ye sailor enough t' know what'll happen if Ah start a brace, wi' this press o' sail oan her? T' wind'ard . . . she goes. Ne'er failed me yet"—a mute caress of the stout taffrail, a slap of his great hand. "Into it, ye bitch! T' wind'ard! T' wind'ard!"

Staggering, taking the shock and onset of the relentless seas, but ever turning the haughty face of her anew to seek the wind, she struggled on nearing the cruel rocks and their curtain of hurtling breakers. Timely, the moon rose, herself invisible, but shedding a diffused light in the east, showing the high summits of the rocks, upreared above the blinding spindrift. A low moaning boom broke on our strained ears, turning to the hoarse roar of tortured waters as we drew on.

"How does 't bear noo, M'Kellar? Is she makin' oan't?" shouted the Old Man.

The second mate, at the binnacle, sighted across the wildly swinging compass card. "No' sure, Sir. . . . Th' caird swingin' . . . think there's hauf a p'int . . . Hauf a p'int, onyway!"

"Half a point!" A great comber upreared and struck a deep resounding blow—"That for yeer half a point"—as her head swung wildly off—off, till the stout spanker, the windward driver, straining at the stern sheets, drove her anew to a seaward course.

Nearer, but a mile off, the rocks plain in a shaft of breaking moonlight.

"How now, M'Kellar?"

"Nae change, Sir! . . . 'bout east, nor'-east . . . deefecult . . . the caird swingin' . . ."

The Old Man left his post and struggled to the binnacle. "East, nor'-east . . . east o' that, mebbe," he muttered. Then to "Dutchy" at the weather helm, "Full, m'lad! Keep 'er full an' nae mair! Goad, man! Steer as ye never steered . . . th' wind's yer mairk. . . . Goad! D'na shake her!"

Grasping the binnacle to steady himself against the wild lurches of the staggering hull, the Old Man stared steadily aloft, unheeding the roar and crash of the breakers, now loud over all—eyes only for the straining canvas and standing spars above him.

"She's drawin' ahead, Sir," shouted M'Kellar, tense, excited. "East, b'nor' . . . an' fast!"

The Old Man raised a warning hand to the steersman. "Nae higher! Nae higher! Goad, man! Dinna let 'r gripe!"

Dread suspense! Would she clear? A narrow lane of open water lay clear of the bow—broadening as we sped on.

"Nae higher! Nae higher! Aff! Aff! Up hellum, up!" His voice a scream, the Old Man turned to bear a frantic heave on the spokes.

Obedient to the helm and the Mate's ready hand at the driver sheets, she flew off, free of the wind and sea—tearing past the towering rocks, a cable's length to leeward. Shock upon shock, the great Atlantic sea broke and shattered and fell back from the scarred granite face of the outmost Stag; a seething maelstrom of tortured waters, roaring, crashing, shrilling into the deep, jagged fissures—a shriek of Furies bereft. And, high above the tumult of the waters and the loud, glad cries of us, the hoarse, choking voice of the man who had backed his ship.

"Done it, ye bitch!"—and now a trembling hand at his old grey head. "Done it! Weathered—by Goad!"

DAVID W. BONE: *The Brassbounder*

BILL ADAMS

Bill Adams was one of the seaman-writers who used to be read much more widely than nowadays. He was a Lime-juice apprentice who settled in California. A good many did, in the old days. Most of them used to run from their ships or, in one of the long periods of depression on the freight market, become bored with the apparent hopelessness of the sea profession. They would get an offer of a job ashore, and they'd go. Two such became famous marine artists—Gordon Grant and Charles Robert Patterson. Several became multi-millionaires.

Bill Adams was no millionaire. He gave himself the fun of life, retired to a mountain village in the Californian Rockies, and led there a simple life, very satisfactory. I called on him there once. It must have been about 1932 or 1933. I recall a big, happy man, soft-spoken, with kindly blue eyes. He lived in a pleasant little home in that mountain village, and it struck me that he was a man who'd had from life just about all he'd asked.

In this extract from his autobiographical *Ships and Women* he writes of joining his first ship.

Ships and Women

Next morning the owner of my ship looked at me from satirical eyes. I didn't like him. A pallid clerk set on the counter before me my apprentice indentures, whereby I was to bind myself to serve the owner for four years with no pay at all.

The said apprentice to furnish all sea bedding and wearing apparel, and faithfully to serve his said Master, his executors, administrators, and assigns; to obey, and keep their secrets; and not absent himself from their service without leave; nor frequent taverns nor ale houses unless upon their business; nor play unlawful games. In consideration whereof the said Master covenants to teach the said apprentice, or cause him to be taught, the business of a seaman and provide him with sufficient meat, drink, and lodging and medical and surgical assistance and to pay said apprentice the sum of thirty pounds.

I took the pen, to sign my name. The owner said, "Better read your death warrant before you sign it." His satirical voice riled me. I signed it, unread.

"I'm going down to the ship. He can come with me," said the owner. Mr Gilson wished me good luck. I followed my owner to the windy street, low dark clouds scurrying overhead. And in a moment, turning a corner, I saw a forest of spars and masts above the warehouse roofs. The wind buffeted us.

"Going to be lively outside, if this keeps up," said my owner, speaking to himself. Outside!—Ah!—Salt water!—*Sailor, sailor, sailor!*

We passed through a gate. Forty years have gone since that morning. But I see her still, just as I saw her then: her stern toward me, on it her name in golden lettering—*Silberhorn*.

Her beauty smote me—sky-pointing masts, low hull, wide tapering spars, perfection of symmetry. And *mine*. Ah—salt water and ships at last! "You'll find it a hard life, my son." I did not think of those words then.

My owner led me along a rope-littered deck on which sails lay outspread. Riggers were aloft, getting her sails up, shouting to one another. Should ever I be able to learn *that* language! My owner led me to a small man amidships, and to him said, "Think you can make a sailor out of this fellow, mister mate?"

The mate glanced at me uninterestedly, looked aloft, and shouted to a rigger. My owner turned and went. A rope falling from aloft dropped heavily on my head and shoulders, knocking my cap off and almost knocking me down. Another, running through a block, tangled my feet. I fell, and rose red-faced. The mate said, "You can come aboard to-night." I was relieved to go ashore.

It was dark when I went aboard again, a porter carrying my sea chest, I with my canvas sea bag on my shoulder—in it my oilskins, sea boots, blankets, tin plate, tin pannikin, tin knife and spoon. I entered a tiny alleyway whence on each side a door opened into a tiny room. The apprentices' half deck, just behind the mainmast. Four lads each side. In each side just room for four narrow bunks, and four sea chests set about a tiny table hinged to the outer bulkhead. I saw the black-haired lad who had asked, "Do you suppose it's as bad as he says?" I saw that other also, and he saw me.

"You damned fool! I told you to go back home!" he said, but spoke with a laugh in his eyes. Glynn Williams, his name was. He had been at sea a year. So had two others, Hickley and Barford. Thompson had served a year in a different ship. Taylor and

Douglas had been for two years in a training ship anchored in the Mersey. Only Wood, the black-haired lad, and I were quite green.

Having had no sleep the previous night, I was very tired. But they sat talking till midnight. Then I was asleep the moment my head touched my pillow. The straw mattress, the "donkey-breakfast", on which I lay was more comfortable than my feather bed at Peterstow had ever been. But in a minute I was awake again. Ten to five of a dark February morning, and my birthday. The watchman was lighting our lamp. He had set a large tin pot on the table. I dressed as did the others, in dungaree jumper and trousers, and drew my sea boots on. No one drank any coffee. I tried to and could not. The pot looked as though it never had been washed. The coffee was bitter well-nigh as aloes.

"Turn to! Wash the decks down!" bawled a surly voice outside. I followed the others to the dim deck, my eyes heavy with sleep.

"Jesus Christ! Wot in hell d'ye think ye are? Get out o' they glad rags!"—the second mate, speaking to Wood, who had dressed in his nice new uniform. He crimsoned, and hurried back to change. Apprentice uniforms are for shore use only.

I was about to roll into my bunk after supper when the mate looked in. "Shift ship!" he said, calm as farmer Jones of Low Cop might say, "Let's us go pick some o' they musharooms."

We moved the ship to the dock nearest the river, to be ready to go out at dawn. No machinery of any sort to help us, we eight lads, with the carpenter and the two mates, dragged on great ropes till nigh midnight—the ship three hundred feet long, by some fifty wide, by twenty-three feet deep in the water. Three thousand tons of cargo in her holds. We were almost done when the crew came aboard. Singing, shouting, cursing, they rolled drunkenly into their quarters in the forecastle, a deckhouse just behind the foremast.

At midnight, my bunk at last. And, blowing the lamp out, Glynn Williams asking merrily, "Who wouldn't sell a farm and go to sea?" Before dawn, "Turn to! Rise and shine! Shake a leg there! No time for coffee this morning."

Wind cried by. Chill rain drove. I mind a muddy river, and lights winking along its shadowy shores. Then a grey tossed sea. Ahead of the tall clipper a tugboat with smoke pouring from her funnels. I don't know how that day passed. Once I saw, on the poop, a man of medium stature, dour-faced, thin-lipped, with eyes that seemed to say coldly one brief word, *"Obey!"*

"That's the damned Old Man," Glynn Williams told me. I'd seen my captain, the skipper.

It was nigh dark when MacDonald, the second mate, dragged from the sail locker two stowaways. Far off a lighthouse winked through the cold evening's scud. As MacDonald came from the locker, each big hand clamped on the neck of a scared young landsman, the Old Man shouted, "Let go the towboat's line!"

Scowling at me as I passed, following the crew up to the fore-castlehead, to let go the line, MacDonald growled, "Ye'd moike a bloodie foine possenger." I had known that a long time since.

The tug came as close as she dared in the tossed sea, maybe fifty or sixty feet from the ship's side. MacDonald tied a rope round a stowaway, hove its other end aboard the tug, shouted, "Haul in!" and lifted and dropped the screaming stowaway to the cold winter sea. The other struggled, too scared for any screaming. But in a minute the tugboat men were hauling him in too. The tug turned on her heel, tooted her whistle thrice in farewell, and was gone. We were free, before us fourteen thousand miles of unfenced salt meadows. I'd forgotten Mr O'Leary and Peterstow long ago. All I knew was a great ache, and hunger also. And yet, too, I was aware of something—aware of a strong majesty in my ship, throwing the sprays high, seeming to challenge the long inrolling ocean swells. No ragged robin now, no meadowsweet, no wood anemone or bluebell. But bronze bells clanging, sonorous across a sullen sea. And, as a sail went threshing and flapping to its masthead, a deep voice singing; and a roar of windy voices coming in on the chorus of my first sea chantey:

"And I give you fair warning before we belay,
    Waye, aye, blow the man down!
And I give you fair warning before we belay,
    Oh, give us some time to blow the man down!
Don't ever take heed of what pretty girls say,
    Waye, aye, blow the man down!
Don't ever take heed of what pretty girls say,
    Oh, give us some time to blow the man down!"

Girls! The word seemed incongruous. I wanted vaseline for my broken blisters, hot food for my hungry young belly, sleep. And, being allowed to go below for supper of skilly and the last dry hash, since I had no vaseline, I rubbed salt-pork grease on my sore palms.

BILL ADAMS: Ships and Women

END OF THE VOYAGE

I come back to Conrad again. His account of the up-Channel run of the ship *Narcissus* is a masterpiece, and the paying-off scene is vivid and real. All sailors knew pay-offs like that when I went to sea.

A week afterwards the *Narcissus* entered the chops of the Channel.

Under white wings she skimmed low over the blue sea like a great tired bird speeding to its nest. The clouds raced with her mastheads; they rose astern enormous and white, soared to the zenith, flew past, and, falling down the wide curve of the sky, seemed to dash headlong into the sea—the clouds swifter than the ship, more free, but without a home. The coast, to welcome her, stepped out of space into the sunshine. The lofty headlands trod masterfully into the sea; the wide bays smiled in the light; the shadows of homeless clouds ran along the sunny plains, leaped over valleys, without a check darted up the hills, rolled down the slopes; and the sunshine pursued them with patches of running brightness. On the brows of dark cliffs white lighthouses shone in pillars of light. The Channel glittered like a blue mantle shot with gold and starred by the silver of the capping seas. The *Narcissus* rushed past the headlands and the bays. Outward-bound vessels crossed her track, lying over, with their masts stripped for a slogging fight with the hard sou'wester. And, inshore, a string of smoking steamboats waddled, hugging the coast, like migrating and amphibious monsters, distrustful of the restless waves.

At night the headlands retreated, the bays advanced into one unbroken line of gloom. The lights of the earth mingled with the lights of heaven; and above the tossing lanterns of a trawling fleet a great lighthouse shone steadily, like an enormous riding light burning above a vessel of fabulous dimensions. Below its steady glow, the coast, stretching away straight and black, resembled the high side of an indestructible craft riding motionless upon the immortal and unresting sea. The dark land lay alone in the midst of waters, like a mighty ship bestarred with vigilant lights—a ship carrying the burden of millions of lives—a ship freighted with dross and with jewels, with gold and with steel. She towered up immense and strong, guarding priceless traditions and untold suffering, sheltering glorious memories and base forgetfulness, ignoble virtues and splendid transgressions. A great ship! For ages had the ocean battered in vain her enduring sides; she was there when the world was vaster and darker, when the sea was great and mysterious, and ready to surrender the prize of fame to audacious men. A ship mother of fleets and nations! The great flagship of the race; stronger than the storms! and anchored in the open sea.

The *Narcissus*, heeling over to offshore gusts, rounded the South Foreland, passed through the Downs, and, in tow, entered the river. Shorn of the glory of her white wings, she wound obediently after the tug through the maze of invisible channels. As she passed them the red-painted light vessels, swung at their moorings, seemed for an instant to sail with great speed in the rush of tide, and the next moment were left helplessly behind. The big buoys on the tails of banks slipped past her sides very low, and, dropping in her wake, tugged at their chains like fierce watchdogs. The reach narrowed; from both sides the land approached the ship. She went steadily up the river. On the riverside slopes the houses appeared in groups—seemed to stream down the declivities at a run to see her pass, and, checked by the mud of the foreshore, crowded on the banks. Further on, the tall factory chimneys appeared in insolent bands and watched her go by, like a straggling crowd of slim giants, swaggering and upright under the black plumets of smoke, cavalierly aslant. She swept round the bends; an impure breeze shrieked a welcome between her stripped spars; and the land, closing in, stepped between the ship and the sea.

A low cloud hung before her—a great opalescent and tremulous cloud, that seemed to rise from the steaming brows of millions of men. Long drifts of smoky vapours soiled it with livid trails; it throbbed to the beat of millions of hearts, and from it came an immense and lamentable murmur—the murmur of millions of lips praying, cursing, sighing, jeering—the undying murmur of folly, regret, and hope exhaled by the crowds of the anxious earth. The *Narcissus* entered the cloud; the shadows deepened; on all sides there was the clang of iron, the sound of mighty blows, shrieks, yells. Black barges drifted stealthily on the murky stream. A mad jumble of begrimed walls loomed up vaguely in the smoke, bewildering and mournful, like a vision of disaster.

The tugs backed and filled in the stream to hold the ship steady at the dock gates; from her bows two lines went through the air whistling and struck at the land viciously, like a pair of snakes.

The stony shores ran away right and left in straight lines, enclosing a sombre and rectangular pool. Brick walls rose high above the water—soulless walls, staring through hundreds of windows as troubled and dull as the eyes of overfed brutes. At their base monstrous iron cranes crouched, with chains hanging from their long necks, balancing cruel-looking hooks over the decks of lifeless ships. A noise of wheels rolling over stones, the thump of heavy things falling, the racket of feverish winches, the grinding of strained chains, floated on the air. Between high buildings the dust of all the continents soared in short flights; and a penetrating smell of perfumes and dirt, of spices and hides, of things costly and of things filthy, pervaded the space, made for it an atmosphere precious and disgusting. The *Narcissus* came gently into her berth; the shadows of soulless walls fell upon her, the dust of all the continents leaped upon her deck, and a swarm of strange men, clambering up her sides, took possession of her in the name of the sordid earth. She had ceased to live.

The men scattered by the dissolving contact of the land came together once more in the shipping office. "The *Narcissus* pays off," shouted outside a glazed door a brassbound old fellow with a crown and the capitals B.T. on his cap. A lot trooped in at once but many were late. The room was large, whitewashed, and bare; a counter surmounted by a brass-wire grating fenced off a third of the dusty space, and behind the grating a pasty-faced clerk, with his hair parted in the middle, had the quick, glittering eyes and the vivacious jerky movements of a caged bird. Poor Captain Allistoun also in there, and sitting before a little table with piles of gold and notes on it, appeared subdued by his captivity. Another Board of Trade bird was perching on a high stool near the door; an old bird that did not mind the chaff of elated sailors. The crew of the *Narcissus*, broken up into knots, pushed in the corners. They had new shore togs, smart jackets that looked as if they had been shaped with an axe, glossy trousers that seemed made of crumpled sheet iron, collarless flannel shirts,

113

shiny new boots. They tapped on shoulders, buttonholed one another, asked: "Where did you sleep last night?" whispered gaily, slapped their thighs with bursts of subdued laughter. Most had clean, radiant faces; only one or two turned up dishevelled and sad; the two young Norwegians looked tidy, meek, and altogether of a promising material for the kind ladies who patronize the Scandinavian Home. . . . The wide-awake clerk called out a name, and the paying-off business began.

One by one they came up to the pay table to get the wages of their glorious and obscure toil. They swept the money with care into broad palms, rammed it trustfully into trousers' pockets, or, turning their backs on the table, reckoned with difficulty in the hollow of their stiff hands. "Money right? Sign the release. There—there," repeated the clerk, impatiently. "How stupid those sailors are!" he thought.

<hr />

At the corner I stopped to take my last look at the crew of the *Narcissus*. They were swaying irresolute and noisy on the broad flagstones before the Mint. They were bound for the Black Horse, where men, in fur caps with brutal faces and in shirt sleeves, dispense out of varnished barrels the illusions of strength, mirth, happiness; the illusion of splendour and poetry of life, to the paid-off crews of southern-going ships. From afar I saw them discoursing, with jovial eyes and clumsy gestures, while the sea of life thundered into their ears ceaseless and unheeded. And swaying about there on the white stones, surrounded by the hurry and clamour of men, they appeared to be creatures of another kind—lost, alone, forgetful, and doomed; they were like castaways, like reckless and joyous castaways, like mad castaways making merry in the storm and upon an insecure ledge of a treacherous rock. The roar of the town resembled the roar of topping breakers, merciless and strong, with a loud voice, and cruel purpose; but overhead the clouds broke; a flood of sunshine streamed down the walls of grimy houses. The dark knot of seamen drifted in sunshine. To the left of them the trees in Tower Gardens sighed, the stones of the Tower, gleaming, seemed to stir in the play of light, as if remembering suddenly all the great joys and sorrows of the past, the fighting prototypes of these men; press gangs; mutinous cries; the wailing of women by the riverside, and the shouts of men welcoming victories. The sunshine of heaven fell like a gift of grace on the mud of the earth, on the remembering and mute stones, on greed, selfishness; on the anxious faces of forgetful men. And to the right of the dark group the stained front of the Mint, cleansed by the flood of light, stood out for a moment dazzling and white like a marble palace in a fairy tale. The crew of the *Narcissus* drifted out of sight.

I never saw them again. The sea took some, the steamers took others, the graveyards of the earth will account for the rest. Singleton has no doubt taken with him the long record of his faithful work into the peaceful depths of an hospitable sea. And Donkin, who never did a decent day's work in his life, no doubt earns his living by discoursing with filthy eloquence upon the right of labour to live. So be it! Let the earth and the sea each have its own.

A gone shipmate, like any other man, is gone forever; and I never met one of them again. But at times the spring flood of memory sets with force up the dark River of the Nine Bends. Then on the waters of the forlorn stream drifts a ship—a shadowy ship manned by a crew of Shades. They pass and make a sign, in a shadowy hail. Haven't we, together and upon the immortal sea, wrung out a meaning from our sinful lives? Good-bye, brothers! You were a good crowd. As good a crowd as ever fisted with wild cries the beating canvas of a heavy foresail; or, tossing aloft, invisible in the night, gave back yell for yell to a westerly gale.

JOSEPH CONRAD: *The Nigger of the "Narcissus"*

STEAMSHIPS

STEAMSHIPS

I WAS never that biased that I was interested only in sailing-ships. It was the obvious adventure of the sailers which attracted me to them, and their poetry and grace. I did not read of steamers when I was young except in the daily Press. Steamships were there, of course. They went about their prosaic work and were taken for granted, as aeroplanes are now. They took the passengers, then the fast freights, then *all* freights from the sailing-ships, but they were an unconscionable time about it. They hadn't driven the last cargo-carrying engineless sailing-ship from the Cape Horn road until 1950.

Now the aircraft are after them.

The steamships had a very hard world to face when first they began and, indeed, for fifty years or more afterwards.

Read, for example, Robert Fulton's own account of some of his difficulties with that allegedly first steamship, the famous *Clermont*, on the Hudson River.

The Fulton Folly

When I constructed my first steam-ship at New York the public took but two views of my enterprise—indifference or contempt. They regarded it as the work of a visionary. My friends were civil, but shy. They listened with patience to my explanations, but with a settled cast of incredulity on their countenances. I felt the full force of the lamentation of the poet,—

> 'Truths would you teach, to save a sinking land,
> All shun, none aid you, and few understand.'

As I had occasion to pass daily to and from the building-yard while my boat was in progress, I have often loitered, unknown, near the idle groups of strangers gathering in little circles, and heard various inquiries as to the object of this new vehicle. The language was uniformly that of scorn, sneer, or ridicule. The loud laugh was at my expense, the dry jest, the wise calculation of losses and expenditure, the dull but endless repetition of 'The Fulton Folly'. Never did a single encouraging remark, a bright hope, or a warm wish, cross my path. Silence was only a cold politeness, to conceal expressions of doubt and reproach.

At length the day arrived when the experiment was to be made (on the Hudson River). For me it was a most trying and interesting occasion. I invited some friends to go on board to witness the first successful trip. Many of them did me the favour to attend, as a matter of personal respect; but it was manifest they did it with reluctance, fearing to be partners of my mortification, and not of my triumph. I was well aware that, in my case, there were many reasons to doubt of my own success. The machinery was new and ill-made, and many parts were constructed by mechanics unacquainted with such work; and unexpected difficulties might reasonably be presumed to present themselves from other causes.

The moment arrived in which the word was to be given for the vessel to move. My friends were in groups on the deck. There was anxiety mixed with fear among them. They were silent, sad and weary. I read in their looks nothing but disaster, and almost repented of my efforts.

The signal was given, and the boat moved on a short distance, and then stopped and became immovable. To the silence of the preceding moment now succeeded murmurs of discontent and agitation, and whispers and shrugs. I could hear distinctly repeated, 'I told you so—it is a foolish scheme. I wish we were well out of it.' I elevated myself on a platform, and stated that I knew not what was the matter; but if they would be quiet, and indulge me for half-an-hour, I would either go on or abandon the voyage. I went below, and discovered that a slight mal-adjustment was the cause. It was obviated. The boat went on; we left New York, we passed through the highlands, we reached Albany! Yet even then imagination superseded the force of fact. *It was doubted if it could be done again, or if it could be made, in any case, of any great value.*

From ROBERT FULTON's own account of the first passage of his pioneer steamer *Clermont* on the Hudson River, the account reprinted in *Ships and Sailors Ancient and Modern*, London 1868.

She had the most terrific appearance from other vessels which were navigating the river. The first steamers, as many in America still do, used dry pine-wood for fuel, which sent forth a column of ignited vapour many feet above the flue, and whenever the fire was stirred a galaxy of sparks flew off, and in the night had a very beautiful appearance. Notwithstanding the wind and tide were averse to its approach, they saw with astonishment that it was rapidly coming towards them; and when it came so near that the noise of the machinery and the paddles were heard, the crews, in some instances, shrunk beneath their decks from the terrific sight, and left their vessels to go ashore, while others prostrated themselves, and besought Providence to protect them from the approach of the horrible monster which was marching on the tide, and lighting its path by the fire it vomited.

American journalist's account of the *Clermont*'s passage, quoted in the same book.

Nothing New

The torpedo, with its unseen and apparently unavoidable means of destruction, was so revolting to the chivalry of our ancestors, that it was regarded as an unfair and cowardly means of attack. But we cannot doubt that it is the duty of every nation to adopt the most successful means for its defence, and can only hope that the contemplation of all "modern improvements" for destruction will act as a deterrent against the deliberate entrance into war.

The torpedo was invented, almost as it remains now, about 1775, by David Bushnall, an American, and employed against the English in the American war. It is thus described in the "Naval Chronicle": "This machine was so constructed as that it could be rowed horizontally at any given depth under water, and could be raised or depressed at pleasure. To this machine, called the 'American Turtle', was attached a magazine of powder, which was intended to be fastened under the bottom of a ship, with a driving screw, in such a way as that the same stroke which disengaged it from the machine should put the internal clockwork in motion. This being done, the ordinary operation of a gunlock at the distance of half-an-hour, or any determinate time, would cause the powder to explode, and leave the effects to the common laws of nature." Two or three of the English vessels were destroyed by this means.

In the same Chronicle for 1808 there is the following:—"About three years ago a man, of grave and mysterious carriage of body, made his appearance in a certain class of fashionable society in London, under the name of Francis. It was shortly whispered about that he was a Yankee American of some consequence, whose real name was Fulton, expatriated for reasons of state." In order to try the effects of Fulton's "submarine bomb", a brig was anchored in the Downs off Walmer Castle. The brig disappeared before the eyes of the astonished spectators, one of whom was Mr Pitt.

Ships and Sailors, 1868

Jet Ship, 1660

The Hydraulic Steamship is a more important invention. This invention really dates back to 1661, but then was a mere idea.

Mr Ruthven, of Edinburgh, began his experiments in 1839, and in 1851 put on the Thames a small vessel, 30 feet long, with the hydraulic propeller.

The invention was brought before the Admiralty, and H.M.S. the *Water-Witch* was chosen for the experiment of hydraulic propulsion. She has engines of 16 horse-power, which turn a huge water-wheel 14½ feet diameter, 8 tons weight. The water required for her work is admitted through holes in the bottom of the vessel to a long iron box, somewhat analogous to the well of a Thames punt, in which gudgeon are kept alive. Then the wheel, put in motion by the steam-engine, sucks in this water, and discharges it with immense force through what we may call the water-guns outside the ship.

The advocates of the new system say that it yields a greater power, in proportion to the fuel consumed, than the old screw and paddle system; that less power is wasted; that the vessel is what the Americans call a "double-ender"; can be driven either backwards or forwards at pleasure, without any stopping or reversing of the engine; and that, in fact, the officer in command can change the ship's course, as well as modify her speed, instantaneously, without communicating with the engine-room at all.

Ships and Sailors, 1868

Jet Ship, 1960

When the new Italian Atlantic liner *Leonardo da Vinci* sails for New York in a few weeks' time, she will have two aluminium emergency lifeboats built in Britain, which are propelled by hydraulic jets instead of propellers. They have been designed by Captain Fleming, founder and head of the Liverpool Company of I. R. Fleming, who pioneered hand-operated propulsion equipment for lifeboats. The boats for the *Leonardo da Vinci* have Gill hydraulic jet propulsion units, powered by air-cooled three-cylinder motors. This sucks in the water through a grilled intake beside the specially perforated deep keel. It then passes it through a double impeller pump, and ejects it through the grill-protected jet which can be revolved through 360 degrees. Several advantages are claimed for this system. One is that a lifeboat can be breasted off sideways from a ship, and another that the jet can also be used to provide a powerful invisible fender of water when coming alongside a ship in a big sea. With an air-cooled engine, it is possible to test the unit while the boat is still on the chocks, and it gives the crew immediate positive control of the boat as soon as it enters the water and is released from the falls.

Press Release, June 1960

THE TITANIC

The loss of the "unsinkable" *Titanic* in the spring of 1912 astonished and alarmed everybody who had anything to do with the sea. More than the *Titanic* went down that April night in a calm, ice-littered North Atlantic. Her loss marked the end of an era—an era when ships went to sea not really regarding lifeboats as fit for the work it was hoped they would never have to perform, and any form of comprehensive lifeboat drill was looked upon as a somewhat offensive way to bore and possibly alarm the passengers. It was an era of carelessness in many other things, too. Perhaps ships had grown up too big too quickly, particularly on the North Atlantic run.

There has been a lot of nonsense written—and filmed—about the unfortunate *Titanic*. Of her senior watchkeeping officers only one—Second Officer Lightoller—survived. Of her engineer officers, none survived. There has been some criticism of these lost officers, especially in books compiled sensationally to become "best-sellers". In charge of the ship when she struck was First Officer Murdoch. He has been criticised, I think most unjustly.

When I went to sea, it was through the aegis of the Ancient Mariners of Victoria. The ship's husband of that society and the moving spirit in helping the boys, was a former White Star officer, Captain Edwin Jones. The White Star Line traded to Australia and New Zealand as well as across the North Atlantic. I remember Captain Jones used to tell the boys, at the hut by Albert Park Lake where he and other "ancient" mariners did what they could to teach us to be handy lads aboard a sailing-ship, how he had shared the bridge of another White Star liner with this same Murdoch, and of his remarkable presence of mind. Here is what he said:

There never was a better officer. Cool, capable, on his toes always—and smart toes they were. I remember one night—we had just come up on the bridge to take over the watch—when the lookout struck the bell for a light on the port bow. It was that awkward moment before you have your night vision, for we had just come up to take over from the First Officer and his junior. Murdoch went at once to the wing of the bridge. I didn't see anything, for a while. I don't think I ever did see that light until it was almost on top of us.

But Murdoch did! And realised on the instant what it was, and precisely what sort of ship was showing it and what she was doing. I never forgot what he did. Before I knew what was happening, he rushed to the wheel, pushed the quartermaster aside, and hung on to the spokes. The First Officer was still on the bridge.

"Hard-a-port!" the First shouted, suddenly seeing the light again, *very* close.

Murdoch kept the ship to her course.

"Hard-a-a-! My God, we'll be into her!" shouted the First Officer. And then: "Midships the helm! Steady! Steady as she goes!"

But Murdoch had not shifted the helm. That was why he had jumped there, fearing a confusion of orders leading inevitably to a collision. As he stood there, coolly keeping our ship on what we all then realised was the only possible collision-free course, a great four-masted barque, wind howling in her giant press of sails, came clawing down our weather side. We watched, horrified. Would she hit us? But she went free. Just, but she went free! It was a matter of yards.

If Murdoch—or the quartermaster at the wheel who of course was there to obey orders and not to question them—had put that wheel over we'd have been into that sailing-ship. We couldn't have helped it. If he had altered to port we'd have hit with our bow: if to starboard, with our stern. Our only chance was to keep our course and speed—to go straight. She was one of the great modern steel windjammers, 3,000 tons of her. She could have cut us down.

We were only two days out of New York at the time. None of us had seen a sailing-ship there before. Remember, even the biggest sailing-ships carried only dim sidelights—oil lamps, generally stuck in towers. They were hard to see. We were looking down: she had a good breeze and was making 12 knots. Under all sail the swelling arch of her foresail would have hidden the sidelight from us. But Murdoch saw—just the one glimpse. It was enough for him. In a split second he knew what to do. We others would have been too late. Upon the instant, he had her figured out! Good thing he did, too.

That man let nobody down aboard the *Titanic*, I'm sure of it.

I quote from the record of the official British Court of Inquiry into the loss of the *Titanic*, held under the presidency of Lord Mersey of Toxteth, with the assistance of numerous highly competent assessors, during May and June 1912. The proceedings were reported more or less verbatim in the shipping papers of the day. My quotations are from the contemporary *Journal of Commerce*, of Liverpool and London.

How the "Titanic" Sank

Robert Patrick Dillon, a trimmer on the *Titanic*, was next called and examined by Mr Raymond Asquith. He was assisting in the engine room in cleaning the gear.

Did you hear the shock when the ship struck?—Yes, and a few seconds before I heard the bell ring.

What happened?—After the ship struck they went slow astern

for about two minutes, then stopped, and then went ahead again.

What did the engineers do when the ship struck?—They went to their stations.

Were the watertight doors closed?—Yes, three minutes after the ship struck.

Did you get any orders?—Yes; we were told to go out of the engine room into the stoke-hold, and we had to lift up the watertight doors to get there.

When you got there what order was given?—To keep steam up.

Subsequently was an order given to draw the fires?—Yes, but I didn't notice in which stoke-hold this was done. I went into four stoke-holds altogether. I returned through the watertight doors to the engine room. This was done to allow the engineers to get to their duties at the pumps in the bow.

Lord Mersey.—Am I to understand that the doors were closed from the bridge and yet the chief engineer told you to open them so as to allow you to pass beneath?—Yes.

How could that be done?—The chief engineer would telephone up to the bridge in order that this might be done.

When you returned to the engine room what happened?—We got the order "All hands on deck."

How long was that after the ship struck?—About an hour and forty minutes.

Did you see any water coming in in the boiler rooms?—Yes, it was coming up through the floors, but there was very little of it.

Where did you go?—I went to the well deck on the starboard side, and heard them singing out "Any more women on board." The last boat was just leaving the ship, and we chased two women up the ladder on to the boat deck.

After that did you see any passengers standing about?—Yes, but no women.

What did you do then?—I went on to the poop.

Who was there?—Some of the crew and passengers, but no women. I waited there till the ship sank.

What did you notice?—The ship plunged and righted herself again, and then went down. I went down with the ship and sank about two fathoms, but rose and was picked up by No. 4 boat. I was swimming in the water about twenty minutes.

Were there any others in the water?—About a thousand, in my estimation.

Did you see any women in the water?—No, sir.

Mr Harbinson.—Had you a lifebelt?—Yes.

Had the passengers lifebelts?—Mostly.

Mr Clem Edwards.—Did you report to anyone in the engine room that water was coming in at No. 4 boiler section?—No; the engineers would see it.

Mr Lewis (for the British Seafarers' Union).—How long were you on the poop?—About 50 minutes.

Could you see the passengers?—Yes.

Was there any commotion?—No; no disorder whatever.

Do you remember when you recovered consciousness in lifeboat No. 4?—Yes; I found a sailor named Lyon and another man lying on top of me, both dead.

Mr Laing, K.C. (for the owners).—You don't know what orders came down to the engine room?—No; I only heard the telegraph ring.

The Attorney-General.—How many of you went from the engine room through these boiler rooms?—Six or seven.

Why didn't you go to No. 5 boiler room?—I had an idea that it was because there was too much water.

Lord Mersey.—Did you think when you were in No. 4 that the reason you were not ordered to go in No. 5 was because there was water in No. 5?—Yes, my lord.

Lord Mersey.—I do not know whether there was any significance in it, but it would appear that the watertight doors that were thus opened by order of the engineer were never closed again.

A Greaser's Story

The Attorney-General (to witness).—You saw the ship sink?—Yes, the forward end went underneath and seemed to break off. The after part came back on a level keel and then turned up and went down.

Was there room on your boat for more people?—Yes. We picked up several men out of the water, including the man Dillon.

Did you see the lights of the *Titanic* as you moved away?—Yes, right up to the end, but they seemed to be going out just then.

Mr Scanlan, M.P.—After you had picked up seven persons had you accommodation for still more people?—For a few more.

Had you sufficient seamen to properly man the boat?—No.

How many men would be adequate?—Ten men.

Had you difficulty all the time in rowing this boat?—Yes.

Had you a boat station given you?—Yes, No. 6.

Have you been on other lines where they have boat drill?—Yes, on the Royal Mail boats.

Mr Scanlan.—Were there enough men in the boat?—No; it would require ten men to man it properly.

Mr Harbinson.—Did you hear any cries?—Not till I got into the boat.

Did you see anyone struggling in the water?—No.

Mr Lewis.—Did you hear a band playing as you left the *Titanic*?—Yes.

From the Attorney-General's Address

One cannot peruse the evidence in this inquiry, continued the Attorney-General, without being struck by the discipline and behaviour of the crew, taken as a whole. In particular there were two of the firemen who went down in the hold knowing the ship was doomed, and stayed there until the water was up to their knees. They remained there till they were ordered to go up on deck by the escape ladder, and they reached the deck only to find that all the boats had gone. Knowing as these men did, all the facts, one is not saying a word too much in saying that their behaviour was heroic. One is also struck with the evidence as to the engineers. Not a single engineer was saved—as Mr Roche said, not an uncommon thing in these accidents. They are right down in the vessel during the time of peril and, as in this case, they don't come up until all hope of saving themselves has disappeared. Another striking fact is that there were eight ship's boys on board this vessel, and every one of them was drowned. They might properly have been treated as juveniles, but they went down as part of the crew of the ship. Really speaking, with the rarest exceptions, in this case everybody on board seems to have behaved in this moment of greatest peril, realising that they were in imminent danger of losing their lives, with a calmness and devotion to duty which I hope will always be remembered to the credit of those who sail in British ships.

One ought also to remember the conduct of the passengers, the accounts given of the women who refused to leave their husbands and take their chance, knowing perfectly well what would happen, and that if they remained they would be doomed to destruction, while the men passengers, with the exception of a rush which was said to have been made for one of the boats on one occasion, also behaved remarkably well. At an early moment it must have been known to all that there was in that vessel only boat accommodation for the women and children, and yet no attempt was made by the men to force themselves into the boats. Even in one case, where two men had got into a boat when there were no women in sight, they got out again when the women came up. It was also shown that though the stewards were called to keep order and see that the women and children only got into the boats, they really had nothing to do, the men passengers making no attempt to get into the boats, and, indeed, assisting the stewards to keep order.

This becomes of greater significance when you present yourself a picture of this ship sinking by the head, the water getting a further and further mastery of the vessel, the boats going away one by one, and the realization of those who remained on board, as the water was getting higher and higher, that at last there would be no boats and no possibility of leaving the ship. There is some evidence that when the news came through that the *Carpathia* was coming Bride, the operator, told some of those on board, and it may be that that caused a good many to remain, but as to this one did not know. One can only surmise that some news of that kind was given, and that it caused those who stayed behind to remain with greater fortitude. Still all the time this vessel is getting nearer to foundering, and all the time the boats are being lowered, and the last means of escaping are disappearing.

A P. AND O. POCKET BOOK

I see by the papers recently, in connection with the promotion of passenger traffic by sea when so much now goes by air, that some steamship companies have been recommending their ships as an antidote for the worn-out aeroplane traveller—an excellent idea. Really, it is a modern variation of an old theme, as the following article in the P. and O. Travellers' Pocket Book for 1888 indicates.

The latest vessel pictured in this passengers' "handy guide" is the *Victoria*, of 1887, and she is shown with two funnels and four masts, the masts all designed to carry sail. I like this extract from the memoranda issued for the guidance of the pursers and stewards-in-charge.

It is your first duty to see a table of superior quality maintained on board your ship, and your passengers thoroughly well satisfied. It has seldom happened, that a really good table was not an economical one, compared with one badly managed. You must clearly understand that what we now instruct you to secure is first an excellent table, and secondly to combine your efforts in that direction with due economy. . . .

The old Pocket Book is full of interest such as its advice to "anyone with six months to spare who wants to pass the time among scenes unaccustomed and interesting to the Western mind" to spend the time in Japan.

"It is not too late to try Japan, but the sooner the journey is undertaken the better," it says. "They do not do things by halves in Japan and, having made up their minds to remodel the ancient Empire upon European principles, they are marching forward with amazing rapidity."

A week is suggested as quite sufficient to see my own home-town, and the advice was probably right.

All this, of course, wasn't any part of my intended sea-faring, though I knew and respected the P. and O. ships in the Australian trade. I had scant prospect of taking passage in any of them.

The Ocean Cure

The great advantage of a sea voyage in cases of ill-health or nervous exhaustion brought about by over brain work, or in cases where comparatively perfect rest is a *sine qua non* for restoration to normal health and vigour, cannot be better treated than in the following extract from the *British Medical Journal*, emanating as it does from the pen of a high medical authority, whose experience has been gained from practical knowledge of life at sea and long residence in hot climates:

"The announcement by the PENINSULAR AND ORIENTAL STEAM NAVIGATION COMPANY of a new and low scale of charges for the highest class of accommodation on their magnificent ships, has a special interest for medical men and their patients. The lowering of the tariff is on return tickets, and is designed to attract passengers who for the purposes of travel or for the recruiting their health may wish to spend some months at sea, varied by excursions on shore in Egypt, India, Australia, China and Japan; and the facilities which are thus afforded to persons of comparatively limited means for obtaining change of scene deserve to be widely known. It is sometimes the subject of reproach to the present generation of medical workers that, whilst rapid strides are being made in the fields of physiology and pathology, the art of therapeutics remains almost stationary. This reproach is not quite justified, even if we limit the healing art to the mere exhibition of drugs; but it fails entirely of justification if we include amongst the means of cure which the physician of the present day has at his disposal, the various ways by which disease can be arrested as well as prevented by simply changing the conditions in which a patient lives. What practitioner is not familiar with the experience that a patient whose life has been long embittered by dyspepsia and hypochondria, for which the Pharmacopœia has found no cure, frequently regains health and happiness by a few weeks' holidays amongst the mountains?

"But whilst the surprising benefit which often follows inland change is universally recognised, it is doubtful whether the equally important therapeutic results that, in many cases, attend a voyage at sea, are sufficiently well known. This ignorance of what may be done for a certain class of patients by prescribing for them an ocean cure, springs from the difficulty which is felt in being able to assure them the care and comfort which the valetudinarian requires; and perhaps also, to some extent, from the want of knowledge regarding the kind of ailments to which it is specially adapted. Amongst the problems which must be worked out in the near future, is that of more accurately defining the class of cases in which the physician may reasonably hope to benefit his patient by sending him to sea, and more especially to be able to advise regarding the latitudes in which he should cruise.

"The benefits of a sea voyage in certain forms of phthisis are so well known that it is needless to enlarge on them, but we doubt whether the majority of medical men are aware of the advantages that sea travel in warm latitudes offers in many other chronic ailments. The passenger, for example, who makes a return voyage to Australia or Japan, is brought under conditions that exercise a powerful alterative influence on his vital condition. They may be shortly enumerated to be the constant breathing of pure air, the exposure to bright sunlight and the free action of the skin—elements in themselves sufficient to effect a rapid cure in many forms of chronic visceral derangements unattended by organic disease. Their effect is nowhere better shown than in certain forms of kidney irritation, which will often, after rendering a patient's life wretched for many months, disappear completely after a few weeks' voyage in the tropics. The powerfully tonic effect of a sea voyage is better understood in the East than it is among ourselves. A patient who has been worn and exhausted by chronic inflammation of the mucous membrane of the lower bowel, left as a sequel of a dysentric attack, will often get rapidly well from the day he leaves port. The inhabitants of these Eastern settlements accustomed to travel, and familiar with the steamships that come to their ports, have learned to recognise in a sea trip a means of regaining health when medicine has failed to help them. Much of these striking results with which medical men practising abroad are familiar, are due to the simple very powerful tonic effect of sea air; and we would in this country be equally familiar with them if our patients could be brought to look on a voyage with less apprehension.

"To the brain workers of our large cities, a voyage at sea offers a form of holiday which is probably unequalled. It is not every middle-aged man to whom the alpenstock, or the grouse moor, or the salmon river is either a source of enjoyment or benefit. Indeed the attempt to recruit an exhausted nervous system by violent muscular exercise unsuitable to a man who has spent the previous nine or ten months in his study or his office, too often leads to an attack of acute disease. To such a man, the rest which a voyage offers to the nervous system can hardly be over-estimated. The restoration of his exhausted energies begins with his first day at sea, as soon as he realises the intense relief of knowing that for a time he has escaped the post-office and the telegraph wire.

"The importance of the bid for the patronage of the increasing number of persons who travel solely for health or pleasure, which is now being made by the well-known Peninsular and Oriental Company, is easily understood by examining their advertisement and prospectus. A passenger may travel on board their vessels about twenty-five thousand miles for a hundred guineas, which is about the sum for which return tickets can be had to Australia, China or Japan. When we consider the large size and comfortable arrangements of the vessels composing their fleet, the safety insured by the tested ability and discipline of their officers, the liberality of their table, and not least, their excellent medical staff, we recognise the importance of the step which the Company have taken in popularising ocean travel"

P. and O. Travellers' Pocket Book, 1888

KENNETH HARDMAN

In these days, one often wonders just what are the attractions of a seafaring career. All the sailing-ships have gone, except for some school-ships and the Portuguese Grand Banks dory-fishing schooners, and both these are somewhat specialised fields. For my own part, I would not have gone to sea if there had not been a square-rigger to go in, and a deep-water-man at that. I often get pathetic letters from youth today imploring me to tell them where they may find such a ship. Kenneth Hardman here, who wrote this little piece for the annual essay competition run by the British Seafarers' Education Service—and won a prize with it—knows his subject. He is a working seaman, and was able seaman in a motorship called the *Diplomat* when he produced this answer.

The Advantages of Seafaring

To be brutally frank, the average modern seaman does not go to sea because he likes the feel of the "blown spume against his face"; nor does he, Masefield-like, revel in the ever-changing moods of the elements on which he sails. I doubt if anyone, a comparative handful of dedicated poets and storm-lovers apart, has ever liked being on the sea (as distinct from being on dry land looking at the sea) in its more violent moods. The indefinable "call of the sea" can and does draw hundreds of lads a year to the training establishments and, ultimately, to the sea—but it cannot hold them there after the first romance and adventure of the thing have worn a trifle thin. Many of them retire, disillusioned, after a few years; others, in this age of conscription, stay on until they are no longer liable for military service, and then slide back into a shore job as gracefully as possible. To the not inconsiderable remainder, the manifold advantages of a seafaring life become

133

more and more apparent as the years go by, until they reach the stage where they begin to wonder how the devil people manage to live permanently ashore at all.

The realisation is gradual and made up of small things. At home, on leave, you notice how so-and-so, who used to sit next to you at school, has aged so obviously that he might almost be taken for your uncle. An isolated case, you think. Then other school-mates and contemporaries pop up, and you see the beginnings of a sedentary paunch here and a factory or machine-shop pallor there. All this is, of course, pure personal vanity; but it is a vanity that everyone possesses in some degree. No one likes to appear to grow old—and it is my steadfast opinion that, as a general rule, seamen retain their youth, both physically and mentally, far longer than their shore-bound contemporaries. I don't really know why; perhaps there's something in this "sea-air" stuff after all.

Another aspect of the personal vanity view, which might be neither readily admitted nor discussed but which is nevertheless still there, is this: the very fact that one is a seaman leads others to recognise that one is a "man of the world", a man who has been places and seen things. An adroitly handled phrase, like "When I passed through the Panama a month ago," can reduce a non-seagoing gathering to something like awe. A man who can speak of a city at the other end of the world with the easy familiarity with which his friends speak of the neighbouring town is definitely not a person to argue with about world affairs.

But these are somewhat nebulous things. The down to earth advantages of a professional sailor's lot are, to a professional sailor, so numerous that it is difficult to know were to begin.

I suppose that, in this mercenary world, the question of money must take first place. Here a seafarer has a unique advantage over a shore wage-earner in that he is practically forced to save a substantial part of his earnings—simply because there is little or no opportunity to spend money at sea. For perhaps nine months of the year, there are none of the expensive diversions of life ashore to worry him. Nor is this too much of a hardship for everyone aboard is, literally and metaphorically, in the same boat. Whilst the landsman decides to stop off at the local for a few beers, or to take the girl friend to a show, the sailor in the middle of the Atlantic blithely and inexpensively plays cribbage, smokes his duty-free cigarettes, yarns with his mates, and turns in.

There are, of course, the "subs." or advances on wages, drawn in foreign parts, but these are seldom very large; and the Old Man usually sees to it that there are not too many of them. The result is quite a substantial pay-off in the home port. Jack, when he does eventually get ashore at home, can usually afford to live at the rate of several thousands a year for the length of his leave—in fact, the rate at which some seamen spend money would probably make many a millionaire blench. There is nothing quite like the good spirits and downright jubilation—known somewhat cynically as the "Channels"—of a homeward-bound crew, with the hard-earned pay-off looming large on the horizon. Whatever trials and tribulations the trip has had to offer, you suddenly feel that it was worth it after all.

The old criticism of life at sea—poor and even bad conditions —is, in the main, no longer valid. Admittedly there are still a few of the older ships where the living accommodation leaves much to be desired, but these can't last much longer, nor will they be the subject of sentimental tears when they do finally end up at the breakers. Almost all the new ships being built now have excellent quarters for every member of the crew. Food and victualling, whilst varying greatly from ship to ship and from company to company, is on the whole pretty fair. It is to be hoped that the days of skimping and saving on ships' catering bills are on the way out.

Many years ago a certain celebrated lady politician is said to have made the statement that seamen should not require payment for their work. The joys of travel, she maintained, should be sufficient in themselves. After all, her friends paid hundreds of pounds in passage money to go to exactly those places to which the seamen went free. There was an obvious flaw in her logic; but, nevertheless, the so-called "wanderlust" has always been a powerful trait in most men. Even the most entrenched bank-clerk or civil servant must at times dream of visiting "far away places with strange sounding names", as a recent popular song puts it. Whilst there are few romantic illusions left for the seasoned sailor—he soon discovers that places and people are much the same the world over—the old thrill of new horizons does not completely desert him. Though he may suspect that Zanzibar will turn out to be the usual conglomeration of flies, heat and stenches, he still watches it grow out of the Indian Ocean with interest. There is always the sense of "going places" about a ship and the very thought of exchanging it for an immovable office or factory is enough to send a shudder through the nautical frame.

How well married life mixes with a life at sea is always a debatable subject. So much depends on the individuals concerned that no hard and fast rule can possibly be laid down. Many men leave the sea when they marry: some through wifely pressure, others because of a natural inclination to be with their wives as much as possible. But many also stay at sea, and are apparently quite happy about it. I read an article in an illustrated magazine recently: the magazine had conducted a survey amongst wives in three classes, or income groups, to discover what job or profession was most conducive to a happy married life in each group. It was the usual hackneyed kind of thing, but the unusual point about it was that, in two of the classes, seamen romped home hands down. The wives concerned gave their reasons—and quite substantial ones they were, too. One said that every time her husband came home it was like a second honeymoon. Another maintained that in nautical marriages there was never time for the couple to get tired of each other: they always tried to look their best and be on their best behaviour to each other during the husband's leaves, all of which it would be well-nigh impossible to keep up indefinitely. All things considered, I believe a seaman can have a happy married life, provided that he confines himself to comparatively short trips. Even the most amenable of wives would be likely to baulk at trips lasting two years or more.

Since time immemorial, the sea has been regarded as a moulder of character. Family black sheep, erring sons, and just plain ruffians, were pushed off to sea as a last resort, the theory apparently being that the sea was an almighty leveller of men, and that they would return home chastened, wiser and better beings. Nowadays the practice is not as popular as it was, but the fact remains that a few years at sea can do wonders for a lad if he has half a mind to avail himself of the unique advantages it offers in the way of self-education. I don't mean education in the scholastic sense—although that is easy enough to come by, too—but in the wider sense of the word: a breadth of mind that comes only with meeting and mingling with people of many races, understanding to the best of your ability their ways of life and viewpoints; and, above all, learning to tolerate that which you cannot agree with nor understand. I have sailed in the fo'c's'les of ships with learned men who never saw the inside of more than a primary school, but they could leave the majority of university graduates standing in their grasp of life and its implications.

Auckland Star

A view no sailor ever had of his Cape Horn ship, from the pilot's window of an aircraft. Here the ill-fated *Pamir* sails a sunlit sea, under all sail. Masefield's *Wanderer* was a similar vessel

United States Coast Guard cadets aloft on their school-ship, the
1200-ton barque *Eagle*, formerly the German naval school-ship *Horst
Wessel*. Cadets on mizzen-mast (in foreground) secure the spanker.
Others on main-mast furl square sail. The *Eagle* makes annual cruises
over the Atlantic and to the West Indies. These are officer-cadets

Cape Horn seamen did not dress like movie stars. Here on the poop of our big *Parma* the sturdy, thick-set Mate, his sea-booted feet apart, the better to maintain his balance, "shoots" the reluctant sun with his own sextant, while (in background) the famous Captain Reuben de Cloux stands beside the teak charthouse. De Cloux won the "Grain Race" from Australia more often than any other ship-master

Traditional way to bring the anchor home aboard big sailing-
ships, but not the traditional crew. These are cadets aboard the
U.S. Coast Guard's barque *Eagle,* straining at her capstan bars.
The capstan is geared to a powerful windlass below decks. Once
round the capstan equals half a link of steel cable home. The *Eagle*
is fitted also with a power windlass for use in emergencies

I sailed in the Indian Ocean, under both the Kuwait flag and the Maldivian, in "dhows" like this 200-ton *baggala* shown beached for cleaning at Kwale Island off Tanganyika. The ornate stern with its five stern windows was copied from the Portuguese. She will float off on the next tide, after her bottom has been "paid" with mixture of fat and lime. I sailed 12 months with the Arabs, a month with the Maldivians

Above

The three-masted schooner *Ana Maria*, lost on the Grand Banks in 1958, was one of the last of the purely sailing Grand Bankers. Deep-laden with salt for the codfish, food and fishing stores she sails from Aveiro, Portugal, on her last voyage. Stacks of flat-bottomed dories almost fill the main deck

Below

Aboard the Portuguese codfishing schooner *Argus* during a bad day on the Greenland banks, 1950. The stacked dories cannot be launched, the dorymen stand-by awaiting better weather. I sailed a six-months' Banks and Greenland voyage aboard the *Argus* which in 1962 still sails

Above
Dory-carrying Portuguese motor-ship alongside at St. John's, Newfoundland, waits for bait in icy Spring. Dories' sails dry in cold sunshine. The Portuguese still—1962— fish by sailing dory on the Grand Banks and west of Greenland, one man to each dory. He sews his own sail, contrives his own rigging, regards the dory as the cowboy does his horse

Right
Antonio Rodriguez of Fuzeta in Southern Portugal—typical doryman of the older school. Here at the wheel of the schooner *Argus*, Antonio has made 40 annual voyages, each of six months. The rest of the year he fishes from his home beaches

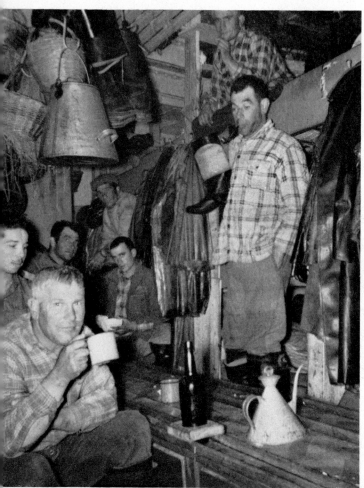

Above
Arctic doryman from the schooner *Argus* "jigs" for cod while his long-line of 600 hooks is down. Ice-blink shows distant coast of Greenland. Dory is already over half-full of cod. Beginning at 4 a.m. the doryman fishes all day, cleans and salts the ship's catch afterwards. The *Argus* carried 55 such dorymen

Left
Crew's quarters called the *Rancho*, in the *Argus*. Dorymen relax over coffee or wine. Bait baskets, sea boots, tea "kettles", oilskins, hang everywhere. Here some 60 men live aboard the 600-ton steel schooner for half a year at a time, catching 800 tons of salted cod

So rests the case for the sea. Doubtless just as many arguments could be made out against the sea as a livelihood, I could find a few myself. It is, as all things are, a matter of personal taste; either you like it or you don't. For myself, I can make no stronger statement than this: if I had a son and he showed the slightest inclination towards a nautical life, he would go away to sea with my blessing.

KENNETH HARDMAN: From the *Seafarer*, journal of the Seafarers' Education Service and College of the Sea, London

LITTLE SHIPS

LITTLE SHIPS

YACHTS and yachting did not normally enter into a working seaman's life when I was young. Paid hands in yachts were a very special class of men in England: in Australia I never met any. The usual Merchant Service seaman knew little of them and cared less.

But he appreciated the beauty and the grace of yachts, the thrill of ocean racing, the delights of long cruising. He liked to read about them, especially in yarns written by a chap who knew his business like Joseph Weston Martyr. Martyr had been at sea under sail himself, in big ships. He knew his stuff. He had a way with a pen, too.

But what I think I liked most was his ability to make voyages which I had always thought fantastically difficult and impossibly expensive to be within the reach, why, of almost everyone.

Like the £200 millionaire.

Lots of sailors I knew in the last of the big sailing-ships dreamt of getting little ships of their own, or talked about it. None ever did, as far as I know. Maybe they failed to accumulate the £200.

From what I saw of them on pay-off days, I could understand that.

The following is from Weston Martyr's story, *The £200 Millionaire*.

My wife and I were sailing a hireling yacht through the waterways of Zeeland last summer, when one day a westerly gale drove us into the harbour of Dintelsas for shelter. A little green sloop, flying the Red Ensign, followed us into port. She was manned solely by one elderly gentleman, but we noted that he handled the boat with ease and skill. It was blowing hard, and the little yacht ran down the harbour at speed, but when abreast of us she luffed head to wind, her violently flapping sails were lowered with a run, and she brought up alongside us so gently that she would not have crushed an egg. We took her lines and made them fast, while her owner hung cork fenders over the side and proceeded to stow his sails. Urged by a look from my wife which said, "He is old and all alone. Help him," I offered to lend the lone mariner a hand. But he refused to be helped. Said he, "Thank you, but please don't trouble. I like to do everything myself; it's part of the fun. But do come aboard if you will, and look round. You'll see there's nothing here that one man can't tackle easily."

We went aboard and found the green sloop to be one of the cleverest little ships imaginable. It is difficult to describe her gear on deck and aloft without being technical; suffice it to say, therefore, that everything was very efficient and simple, and so designed that all sail could be set or lowered by the man at the helm without leaving the cockpit. The boat was 30 feet long by 9 feet wide, and my short wife, at any rate, could stand upright in her cabin. Her fore end was a storeroom, full of convenient lockers, shelves and a small but adequate water-closet. Abaft this came the cabin, an apartment 12 feet long, with a broad bunk along one side of it and a comfortable settee along the other. A table with hinged flaps stood in the middle, while in the four corners were a wardrobe, a desk, a pantry and a galley. Abaft all this was a motor, hidden beneath the cockpit floor. A clock ticked on one bulkhead, a rack full of books ran along the other, a tray of pipes lay on the table, and a copper kettle sang softly to itself on the little stove.

"What do you think of her?" said our host, descending the companion. "Before you tell me, though, I must warn you I'm very houseproud. I've owned this boat for ten years, and I've been doing little things to her all the time. Improving her, I call it. It's great fun. For instance, I made this matchbox-holder for the galley last week. It sounds a trivial thing; but I wish I'd thought of it ten years ago, because during all that time I've had to use both hands whenever I struck a match. Now I have only to use one hand, and you know all *that* implies in a small boat, especially if she's dancing about and you're trying to hold on and cook and light the Primus at one and the same moment. Then there was the fun of carving the holder out of a bit of wood I picked up, to say nothing of the pleasure it gives me to look at a useful thing I've made with my own hands. The carving brought out the grain of the wood nicely, don't you think? Now I'm going to make tea, and you must stay and have some with me."

142

We did stay to tea. And we are glad we did. For one thing, it was a remarkably fine tea, and, for another, we listened to the most entertaining and thought-provoking discourse we have ever heard in our lives.

"Do you live aboard here all alone *always?*" exclaimed my wife, making her eyes very round.

"Most certainly," replied our host. "Now do try some of this Macassar redfish paste on your toast. I got it in Rotterdam from the purser of the Java Mail that arrived last week, so it's as fresh as it's possible to get it."

We had some more tea. It was a marvellous brew, as stimulating as good wine, and while we drank it our curiosity concerning our host and his extraordinary mode of life welled up within us, to drown at last our manners and overflow in a stream of questions.

"Do you really mean," said we, "that you live aboard here always? All the year round? And quite alone? And cruise to Odessa? And Warsaw? And how did you *get* to the Danube? And the Black Sea? And ——? And ——?" Thus we went on, while our host smiled at us—the kind of smile that told us we had made a new friend.

"I'll tell you," he said, when we stopped at last for breath. "You understand boats and this sort of life, I think, so you'll understand me. I've been living aboard this boat for ten years now, and I hope I shall never have to live anywhere else as long as I'm alive. It's a good life. It's the best kind of life a man can lead—or a woman either. It really is *life,* you see. Yes. And I think I ought to know. I shan't see sixty again, and I've seen a good deal of life—of different kinds. I'm a doctor, or was once. And I've worked very hard all my life trying to be a good doctor, but failing, I fear, on the whole. I married and we had five children, and it meant hard work bringing them up properly and educating them. But I worked and did it. Then I moved to London to try to make some money. This was the hardest work of all. Then the war came, and more hard work in a base hospital. The war killed two of my sons—and my wife. And when it was all over I looked around, and I didn't like the look of the life I saw ahead of me. To go on working hard seemed the only thing left to do, but I found there was no zest left in my work any more. My daughters were married and my remaining son was doing well in a practice of his own. I found my children could get on very well without me. So there was no one left to work for, and I found I was very tired.

"I sold my practice and retired—to Harwich, where I was born. And there I soon found out that having nothing to do at all is even worse than working hard at something you've lost interest in. I did nothing for six months, and I think another six months of that would have been the death of me. . . . But this little boat saved me. I began by hiring her from a local boatman for one week-end. We sailed up the Orwell to Ipswich and back again. The weather was fine, the Orwell is a lovely river, and I enjoyed my little sail. I enjoyed it so much, in fact, that I hired the boat again. I hired her for a week, and this time I left the boatman behind and sailed alone. Of course, I had sailed boats before. As a boy I got myself afloat in something or other whenever I had a chance, and my holidays as a young man were nearly all spent aboard yachts. So I found I could still handle a boat, especially this little thing in those sheltered waters, and I remembered enough seamanship to keep myself out of trouble. . . . After that I grew bolder, and one fine day, with a fair wind for the passage, I coasted along the Essex shore to Brightlingsea. I explored the Colne and its creeks, and the end of my week found me at West Mersea, so I had to write to the boatman and extend the time of hire. While I was about it I chartered the boat for a month. You see, I discovered I was happy, and I could not remember being happy for a very long while. The exercise and the fresh air and the plain food were all doing me good, too.

"My month was up almost before I knew it, and when it did get time to go back to Harwich and all *that* meant, I simply could not bear the thought of it. . . . I had just enough means to allow me to live, very simply, and even the expense of hiring this boat was really more than I could afford. What I wanted to do, of course, was to go on living aboard her, but, to my sorrow, that seemed quite impossible.

"Then, one night, I sat down in this cabin and thought the thing out—right out, in all its bearings. First I considered the question of finance. I don't want to bore you with my private affairs, but the figures are, I think, instructive and valuable, as they show what a lot can be done with very little. My capital amounted to a little over £4,000, and my yearly income just touched £200. The problem I set out to solve was: can I buy the boat out of my capital and still have sufficient income to live aboard her all the year round, and to maintain the boat and myself adequately? The price of the boat I knew already; she was for sale for £200. If I bought her my income would be reduced to £190, or less than £16 a month. Was this enough? It did not look like it, by any means. It meant only £3 17s. a week to cover food, clothing, light and heat, and upkeep and repairs to the boat, to say nothing of depreciation and insurance. The figure seemed so ridiculous that I nearly gave up my idea in despair.

"However, I am, thank goodness, a methodical sort of man, and I'd kept a list of my expenses during the time I'd been living aboard the boat. I analysed that list and found that my food and oil for the lamps and stove had cost me only £7 15s. for the month. I had also spent 30s. on gear for the boat, such as paint, ropes, shackles and such things, while my bill for petrol and lubricating oil came to 15s. only, as I had sailed as much as possible and used the motor as little as I could. Not counting the cost of hiring the boat, my total expenditure had, therefore, been only £10 for the month, or £120 a year. This left £70 over for repairs, accidents, depreciation and insurance. As far as the finance was concerned, the thing began to look possible after all.

"I was very cheered by this discovery, and I then asked myself: 'Can I continue to live aboard this little boat from year's end to year's end in health and comfort of body and mind?' As far as the summers were concerned I knew I could answer that with a whole-hearted 'Yes'. But what about the winters? Could I endure being shut up in a small confined space while the gales blew and it was cold and wet, and the nights were long and dark? I wondered. And I had to admit to myself, very much against the grain, that I probably would not be able to endure these things. I remember I went to bed after that, feeling very miserable. But when I woke up next morning the first thing I said to myself was, 'But why stay in England in the winter? Why be cold and wet when all you have to do is to follow the sun and sail your boat— your Home—south?'

"To cut all this short, I sailed back to Harwich and sent to London for a map of the French canals. And when it came I found my idea of following the sun south was entirely feasible. All I had to do was to choose a fine day in early autumn and sail across the Channel from Dover to Calais. From Calais the map

145

showed me a network of canals and navigable rivers spreading over the whole face of France, and I discovered that a boat of this size and draught could proceed through those inland waterways right through the heart of France to the Mediterranean. I bought this boat that same day. I had a few small alterations made to her, and the following week I sailed from Harwich, bound south— for Ramsgate, Dover, Calais, Paris, Lyons, and the Riviera."

"Well done!" I cried. And my wife said, "Hush! And then? Then?"

Our new friend smiled at us again. "Yes," he said. "You're right. It was a bit of a rash proceeding—at my age. But I've never regretted it. That first cruise was perfectly delightful and, on the whole, a very simple affair. I had my troubles, of course. . . . I stayed in Dover for ten days before I judged the weather was fine enough for me to sail to Calais. The truth is, I was rather scared. The passage is only twenty-one miles, but I felt a regular Christopher Columbus when I ventured across the Channel at last. It was a fine day, with a light north-east wind, and under sail and motor I got across in four hours. I assure you Columbus was nothing to me when I sailed into Calais harbour! I felt I had triumphantly accomplished a most tremendous adventure, and I was immensely pleased and proud. And I can assure you it's rather remarkable for anything to make a cynical and disillusioned old man of my age feel like that. . . .

"I wandered down the Oise to Paris, where I stayed a week, moored in the Seine almost in the shadow of the Champs-Elysées' trees. It was amusing and comfortable, too, living in the middle of Paris like that. I could dine ashore if I wanted to and go to a theatre, and then walk back and go to bed in my own little floating hotel without any fuss or bother. And when I got tired of the city I just moved on, hotel and all. I went up the Marne to Chalons, along the canals to Bar-le-Duc and Epinal, and down through the Haute Saône and Côte d'Or country to Mâcon and Lyons. I mention these towns to show you the route I took, but it was all the little out-of-the-world places between them that I used to stop at and which I found so interesting. I met all sorts of people and everyone was very helpful and kind, and by the time I got to Lyons I could speak about four different brands of French quite well.

"I found myself looking forward to each day, and every day had some new interest. Life nearly was, without exaggeration, perfect. If I found myself anywhere or amongst people I did not care

146

for, all I had to do was to heave up my anchor and go somewhere else. That's one of the many advantages of living aboard a boat. When you want to go away there's no packing, no taxis, no tips, no trains and no bother. And you haven't got to find a place to lay your head when you get to your journey's end. In a boat you just move on, and your sitting-room, your kitchen, your bedroom and all your little personal comforts and conveniences move on with you. And when you get to your destination there you are—at Home.

"It added to my peace of mind, too, to find I was living well within my income, in spite of the fact that I was living very well and doing myself a great deal better than I had, for instance, in my Harwich lodgings. Of course I had to be careful and not go in for too many luxuries, but I lived as I wanted to live, and it surprised me to find how little it cost me to do it. I'll show you my account book, if it will interest you, but first I'll show you where I've been during these last ten years.

"Look at this! It's the official French canal map, showing all the canals and navigable rivers in the country. You'll notice there's very little of France you can't get at by water. It's almost unbelievable where you can go; everywhere, practically, except to the tops of the mountains. It's the same in Belgium and Holland, and in Germany, too, and until I got these canal maps I had no idea of the extraordinary manner the inland waterways of Europe have been developed. The ordinary maps don't give the details, so perhaps it's not surprising that people in England don't realise they can travel in a yacht from Calais through every country in Europe, except Spain and Italy, entirely by river and canal. It sounds incredible, doesn't it? But I've done it myself, in this boat. Including Switzerland!"

"Switzerland!" cried my wife. "How *did* you?"

"There are two ways of getting there," said our extraordinary friend. "Up the Rhine Lateral canal, or the way I went—up the Rhine-Rhone canal from Strassburg to Mulhause and along the Huningue canal to Basle. . . . I spent a summer cruising up the coast to L'Orient and from there along the canals, right through Central Brittany from Brest to Nantes. Then I came south again, away from the cold, and spent the winter exploring South-West France, along the Dordogne and the Garonne and its tributaries."

I remember it was at this point in our friend's discourse that I interrupted him by crying out in a loud voice, "By God!" and hitting the cabin table hard with my fist. My wife said nothing, but there was a look in her eyes and a light in them that showed me she understood and approved the wild and fascinating thought that had flashed into my mind. And our friend, it appeared, understood me also, for he said, "Yes. Why not? All you need is a boat drawing less than four feet, with a motor in her for choice and her mast in a tabernacle. That and the—well, let's call it courage; the courage to step out of your rut. It looks hard; but a mere step does it—as I found out. Of course, it costs money. Following the seasons all over Europe in your own home is a millionaire's life; but I've managed to live it at an average cost, over the last ten years, of less than £150 per annum. Look at this!"

He put an open book before us on the table. It was his account book, and it contained, in full detail, his daily expenditures during all the years he had been living aboard his boat. It was, I can assure you, a most engrossing work, and was full of items such as these, which I found on a single page and copied there and then. And I shall regret it till I die that I had no time to copy more:

Sept. 5. Capdenac. 8 duck eggs and 1 duck (cooked), 3s. 1d. *7th.* 10 lb. grapes in fine willow basket, gratis. 6 boxes matches, 2s.! Sulphur at that! Note: Smuggle in big stock of matches when next I come to France. *8th.* Very hard cheese, 1 ft. in dia., 1 basket peaches, 1 jeroboam peach brandy, 1 kiss on both cheeks, gratis, or perhaps fee for removing flint from farmer's eye. *9th.* Mule hire, 10d. Alms to leper, 1s., interesting case. Castets, *15th.* 6 feet of bread, 1s., 1 pint turps, ½d. *16th.* 2 gallons turps, 8d. Castelsarrasin, *Oct. 2nd.* Bribe to gendarme, 5d. I should dearly like to publish that account book, just as it stands, without any comment or explanation. It would, I think, make fascinating and suggestive reading.

"Look here," said our friend, turning over the unique pages and exposing the following figures to our devouring eyes. "This is a summary of my first twelve months' income and outgoings:

Income: £190 0 0	Expenditure: Upkeep of boat (at 9s. per week)	£23 8 0
	Petrol and oil (distance covered under motor, 1,220 miles)	10 4 0
	Charts, canal dues	13 8 0
	Food, drink, clothes, light and heat (at just under £2 a week)	100 0 0
		£147 0 0
	Balance	43 0 0
		£190 0 0

"I managed to save £43, you see, that first year—enough to buy a new boat like this one, every five years, if I continued to save at the same rate. I was extra careful that year. I didn't spend much on myself, but I bought the boat all she needed and kept her up in first-class shape. . . . My fuel bill was very small, because I never use the motor if I can sail. The £13 odd for dues, &c. was mostly spent on maps and charts, not that many charts are necessary, but I simply can't resist buying the things. I spend hours poring over them, and planning more voyages than I shall ever have time to make. As for the canal and harbour dues—they're ridiculous; generally some fraction of a penny per ton. And this boat's registered tonnage is only two ton. The only expensive piece of water to travel over in Europe is the Rhone. It's got a terrific current, pilotage is compulsory, and to get up it you have to be towed. Everywhere else the only trouble about the charges is to find change small enough to pay them with. £2 a week for food and so on sounds very little, but all I can say is I live well on that sum. You see, if I want, say, vegetables, I don't go to a shop in a city for them. No. Perhaps I see a good-looking garden on the river bank. I stop and have a yarn with the owner, and when I depart I'm the richer by a basket full of fresh vegetables, and maybe a chicken and some eggs and fruit as well, while the gardener is left with a fair price for his produce and something to talk about for weeks. He's pleased and I'm pleased. . . .

"Clothes don't bother me much. It's not essential to dress in the latest style. I keep my go-ashore clothes in that tin uniform case, and when I get to a city and want to see the sights I put on a civilised suit. Otherwise I use soft shirts, jerseys and flannel trousers. I do my washing myself; half an hour a fortnight does it, which is nothing to grumble about. I use paraffin for light and cooking in the summer, and in the winter I keep that little stove going on coal and wood. I find I burn wood mostly, because I've got a passion, apparently, for collecting any odd pieces I find drifting about. There must be a strain of longshoreman blood in me somewhere, I think, for I can't resist picking up bits of driftwood, even though I have to throw most of them overboard again, and I generally have a bigger collection of the stuff on deck than I can ever hope to burn.

"So you see, one way and another, my expenses are very small. The £30 or £40 I save every year I put by for accidents, major repairs, depreciation and a sort of insurance fund. I've bought a new suit of sails and had the whole boat surveyed and recaulked and the engine practically renewed, all out of the fund, and I've still got enough left to buy a new boat if I want one. I'm getting so rich, in fact, that I don't know what to do with all my money. I tried to get rid of some of it by buying extra fine gear for the boat, but I found that scheme merely saved me more money in the long-run."

Said our friend, "I've found one good way to live and be happy. There must be other ways, too, but I don't know 'em, so I mean to stick to my way—till I come to the end of it. The secret seems to be, to do everything you can *yourself*. It's difficult to explain, but take an example. Take travel. Allow yourself to be carried about the world in Wagon-Lits and cabins-de-luxe, and what do you get out of it? You get bored to death. Everything is done for you and you don't even have to think. All you have to do is to pay. You're carried about with the greatest care and wrapped up and fed and insulated from—from everything. You see about as much of life as a suckling in the arms of its nurse. No wonder you get bored! But get yourself about the world, on your own feet, or in your own boat, and you're bound to fill your life with interest and charm and fun—and beauty. You'll have your disagreeable and uncomfortable times, of course, but they merely serve to make the good times taste better. 'Sleep after toyle, port after stormie seas ——.' Old Spenser knew. He'd been through it."

Next morning our friend must have risen with the sun, and we were still beneath our blankets when the incense of his coffee and bacon drifted down our cabin hatch. Presently the sound of ropes falling on deck warned us he was getting under weigh, and we arose to say good-bye to him. "Good morning," said he, "I'm sorry to disturb you so early, but I want to catch the first of the flood. With luck it'll carry me into the Rhine and I'll be in Germany by evening. Now I'll cast off and go—and see what this good day's got in store for me. A fair tide and a fair wind is a fine beginning, anyway. Good-bye, you two. We'll meet again somewhere, for certain, if only you follow that impulse you had last night. I don't want to influence you unduly; but, remember —one step does it and you're out of the rut for good. Good-bye. God bless you both."

He set his jib and the little green yacht fell off before the wind and headed for the harbour entrance. She sailed away with the sun shining bright upon her, and upon the white head of the man at her helm. Presently she entered the broad river, and we saw our friend look back and wave his hand in farewell. Then the boat was hidden by a bank of golden sand, and the last we saw of her was her little Red Ensign, a tiny flame outlined against the sky.

This seems to be the end of the story—but I do not know. I am not sure. I am not sure, because the words of that elderly adventurer seem to have set us thinking. I notice we do not say very much, but I know we think a lot. For, at intervals during the cold and fogs of this last winter, there have passed between my wife and me some detached but significant utterances—such as: "I don't see why I couldn't get on with my writing aboard a boat just as well as I can inside this flat."

"Only £200 a year! Hang it! We *ought* to be able to earn that much between us, you'd think?"

"I think, my dear, one of those steam-cookers would be a splendid thing to have if we—for anyone living aboard a small boat."

"What a foul fog! It hurts to think of the sun shining, *now*, in the south of France."

"May the Devil run away with that damned loud-speaker next door. You know, if this flat was a boat, we could move it out of hearing."

"If I get bronchitis again next winter—My dear, I don't think I *could* stand another winter here."

Also we have purchased a monumental work entitled, "Guide Officiel de la Navigation Intérieure," published by the Ministère des Travaux Publiques. This is a fascinating work, heartily to be recommended. It has a lovely map.

Also we have just heard of a little boat. In fact, we have been to look at her. She is sound and very strong. She has two good berths and a galley and lots of stowage space. Also she has a little auxiliary motor. And her mast is in a tabernacle. And she is for sale. And we have fallen in love with her. So perhaps this is not the end of this story. In fact, we hope and we pray this story has only just begun.

WESTON MARTYR

ADVENTUROUS COCKLESHELLS

I don't know about following Weston Martyr's idea, but the number of odd craft and small vessels of all kinds sailing on long voyages about the seas today is incredible. Previous generations were unable to do that sort of thing on quite the same scale. £200 a year would not really go very far. In the Melbourne of my childhood, the memory of Captain Joshua Slocum's call there in the tiny *Spray* was still fairly recent, and the old Blue Nose was spoken of with astonishment. But it was a long, long time before anyone followed in his wake.

Daring voyages in minute vessels were nothing new in Australian waters. The story of our discovery and early history was full of them—the pioneers Bass and Flinders in their tiny *Tom Thumb*, a cockleshell eight feet long in which they discovered and surveyed along the coast of New South Wales, the same George Bass again in an open whaleboat sailing 600 miles to Westernport in Victoria discovering Bass Straits (a rough stretch of water, if ever there were one!), the redoubtable Captain Kelly's circumnavigation of Tasmania in another cockleshell—these voyages we learned of at primary school, and admired.

Our countrymen had been accustomed from the earliest days to go off down the sealing islands of the Roaring Forties and the Screaming Fifties in wild south latitudes, after sealskins, blubber, penguins, mutton-birds, anything that could be converted into coin. A more sinister citizenry had used any sort of thing that would float to escape—escape anywhere, preferably the South Seas.

The cockleshell voyage was therefore nothing new. It was the idea of such voyages as an adventure for their own sake that was new. Slocum was remembered as a rather kindly but eccentric old seafaring vagabond. He had an Australian wife, and some children somewhere, hadn't he? What about them? He was a shipmaster: there were still plenty of sailing-ships. Why wasn't he employed? The Australian in those days was apt to take a strictly practical view: in so vast a land, and hard, where a second-generation local was aware of the tradition of the arrival of his parents in some gold-rush little brig, nobody had much chance or inclination to make long voyages in yachts. Beachcombers made for the tropic isles of the Great Barrier Reef or the luscious South Seas, where they were not usually regarded as estimable characters.

In recent years, that has changed: Australians, like most others, wander the world in all sorts of vessels—even in an amphibious jeep—or, now that real sailing-ships go there no longer (since no such ships are left), make towards the Horn in yachts. Yachts race from Sydney to Hobart in Tasmania, where once Bass and Flinders sailed. Yachts race the Tasman Sea, a nasty place much cursed by sudden storms.

These modern yachts are very much more seaworthy vessels than Bass and Flinders had, or Captain Kelly and his kind. A sound and properly maintained modern yacht carrying her class at Lloyd's should be able to go anywhere. A good many do.

Hardly a week goes by, even nowadays, when I don't get at least one letter from some would-be lone navigator, asking for advice—though I'm no lone mariner, and never have been. Anything with a waterline length of less than fifty feet doesn't suit me at all, for life aboard those cockle-shells is a feat of endurance. Now why does a man want to go off sailing around the world by himself? I've often wondered.

I've seen a good many of these chaps, one place or another. I remember calling in at Tahiti, with the *Joseph Conrad*, when I was on the way round the world myself. (She was a full-rigged ship, and I was not alone.) There were seven or eight midget circumnavigators tied up along the Papeete waterfront. One of them was a retired schoolmaster who'd come down from California in a bit of a thing about twenty-four feet long, that I'd have hesitated to take along the Isis at Oxford. How much further he went I don't know, but he said he was going round the world. The last I saw of him his ship was still tied up alongside and he'd taken a house ashore, but he declared that was only an interlude. There were a couple of young Norwegians there, too, and three different collections of American college boys.

I remember those Norwegians. They'd been nearly three years on the road then. Their custom, as far as I could make out, was to call in at some island—any island—and stay until they had absolutely worn out their welcome, and in some of the islands, that took some time. They'd been six months at one place, they told me—Norfolk Island, I think it was—and at last the citizens implored them to leave. They loved having them of course, for the young fellows were delightful company, and they played the guitar very nicely. But if the harsh truth has to be told, they didn't really make any secret of the fact that they were just a couple of beachcombers with a boat. They hadn't any funds whatever, and no intention of getting any.

In the early days of these wandering yachts in the Pacific, a Union Steamships mail steamer on the San Francisco to Sydney run came across one somewhere near Tahiti. There was only one chap aboard and he was sound asleep at the time. So, thinking he was a castaway, the mail steamer picked him up and took him on to the next port, leaving his little vessel to flounder on alone. The lone mariner, of course, raved and shouted and yelled to be left in his boat. But they thought he had a touch of the sun and they didn't believe him. They believed him all right when, later on, he sued the line for damages for piracy! He got the damages, too.

As for sailing alone, the trouble is that it's a rare pair of fellows who get along so well that they really are able to share a circumnavigation in a small ship. Three or four might manage, but very rarely two. It *seems* easy enough. But it is not. It's far better to be alone—or take your wife, and nobody else. The best two-piece crews I've ever come across have been man and wife. But you've got to remember that it's asking a lot of a wife. The mere physical throwing around that you have to put up with in anything at all like bad weather is enough to wear down the average strong man. The sea just won't stay quiet, and it has to be very, very quiet if the motion of a small boat isn't excessive. Even hardened old salts can get very seasick in small yachts, and there's no truth in the landsman's belief that if you do get sick once on a voyage and get over it, you're immune at least for the remainder of that voyage.

The Best Crew

This seems to be the season for adventurers who like to buck the sea for the fun of it. For instance, Lieutenant Commander Edward Atkinson and Able Seaman Fred Fisher reached home during 1959 after sailing a 24-foot sloop from Singapore. They'd spent just over 200 days at sea in the craft, which Commander Atkinson built himself. The same year saw the end of an even tougher venture when two women and a man came ashore at Dun Laoghaire—the port for Dublin—after their *second* Atlantic crossing in a home-built catamaran. The story goes back to the middle of 1955 when Jim Wharram, of Manchester, built himself a catamaran of two 23-foot floats linked by two crossbooms with a tiny deck, and recruited as crew two German women he met working on a Yorkshire farm. In September 1955, he sailed out of Falmouth in his strange craft, which he called *Tangaroa* after a Polynesian sea-god.

The *Tangaroa* reached the Canary Islands all right, and Jim stayed there with his two-women crew for a year before setting sail for the West Indies. When they reached Trinidad, the *Tangaroa* was holed on a reef, but they managed to paddle her ashore. Then this strange seafaring trio went to New York and built another catamaran they called *Rongo*. Their homeward voyage from New York took them seven weeks instead of four—and the catamaran had a tough time in the gales. Commenting on the composition of his crew, Mr Wharram who is 31 years old said: "I think three men in a boat would get on each other's nerves. Two men and one girl would also be a strain. My crew is sensibly proportioned."

From a B.B.C. General Overseas Broadcast (for the Merchant Navy) Oct. 8, 1959.

I receive a good many letters like the following, spelling and all, which came in the other day. There didn't seem much sense in answering it.

A School-boy's Letter

Dear Sir.

Would please give my friend and myself some advice on what kind boat to buy, as we are thinking of sailing to Austrailia. The boat we have at the moment is an exships life boat converted, 32 ft. long, 12 ft. beam, draught 3-4 ft. I my self think its a tall order for a boat that size, thought its been done in one's small than ours.

We dont have much idear on Navigation at sea, but then Dwight Long and others didnt eighter. We have taked it over now for almost six months, and relise what we are letting our selfs in for, also we have seen the sea in calm's and in rough weather and know what it can do. We would be glad to recive your advice on this subject and on what charts ects. to have.

The only advice I could possibly offer was that given by Punch to those about to marry. Don't! But they do, just the same. I haven't heard of this particular converted ship's boat again, but there have been others. Like the following, for instance.

Lone Voyager's Death at the Solomon Islands

Tulagi, Oct. 15

The end of a long adventure came a few weeks ago when the *Chance*, a converted lifeboat, which was doing one of the long single-handed adventure trips which are now one of the few remaining outlets for the spirit of discovery and self-reliance that persists in man, drifted into Kia Passage, Ysabel, with the body of a man of 72 years, apparently dead some days.

So far as is known here, the adventurer was an American, and had contributed articles to various newspapers on his experiences. Probably he would have asked no better ending to his voyage or his life, than to pass away in the midst of his travels. Up to the present time the vessel has not been brought into Tulagi.

Pacific Islands Monthly, November 1935

Kayak Across the North Atlantic

New York, Jan. 30

The story of a remarkable voyage across the Atlantic at its stormiest time, in a craft so frail in appearance that one would have thought it unlikely to outlive even a moderate storm, was told today in the *New York Times*.

It is the account by Dr Hannes Lindemann, a doctor of Hamburg, of his journey of 3,000 miles in 72 days, beginning on

October 20, from Las Palmas in the Canary Islands to St Martin in the Lesser Antilles, in a sort of kayak.

This boat, 17 ft. long, was made of rubberized canvas stretched over a wooden frame, and contained air tubes for buoyancy. It had, beside the main sail, two small square sails—one rigged forward, the other aft on a short mizzen mast. With no room in it to lie down, Dr Lindemann had to snatch what sleep he could sitting up.

"I capsized twice in storms," he said. "The first time was on the fifty-seventh day out, I lay on the overturned boat until the storm went down, then righted her and baled out. However, I had lost most of my provisions, and my sextant and chronometer soon rusted to uselessness. The second time was two days later, but that accident was only 10 minutes."

This Dr Lindemann had already crossed the Atlantic in a West African dugout canoe. He wrote a book about his voyages called *Alone at Sea* (Random House, New York, 1958).

By Rowing Boat

Back in the spring of 1896 two Norwegians, George Harbo and Frank Samuelson, decided to row from New York to Havre, France. In a double-ender something between a New Bedford whaleboat and a dory, they started off amid the most doleful predictions. They capsized off the Grand Banks, losing their stove and most of their provisions. Twice they fell in with sailing-ships, which obligingly gave the rowers a hot meal and a new supply of water and grub. Fifty-four days from New York they landed on the Scilly Islands, off Cornwall, England; and, after a few days' rest, rowed on to Havre. (Details vouched for by Harold L. Seaman, a Jersey boatbuilder whose grandfather built the craft that made the trip, and by clippings from the New York *Tribune*.)

The Sportsman

There is a column in *Lloyd's List*, the daily publication of the great insurance house of Lloyd's in London, which gives reports of sighting of odd vessels which have no W/T with which to report themselves. Years ago, the list was often a long one, when a group of sailing-ships got themselves becalmed on some shipping lane. Today it is usually limited to odd tidings of small yachts on ocean passage and, as these do not get on shipping lanes much, it is usually brief.

The list is headed "Speaking", for a very good reason. The ships have been spoken to.

Some odd craft get in the Speaking Column from time to time. Here are a couple:

A yacht, 30 to 40 ft. long, white sail, one man in cockpit, no name, or signals, heading south-westerly, Mar. 4, 6.45 p.m., G.M.T., lat. 25 49 N., long. 16 22 W., by *Rippinghame Grange* at Las Palmas.

Lloyd's, London

L'Hérétique, rubber raft, Doctor Bombard expedition, all well, Dec. 10; lat. 15 38 N., long. 49 50 W., by steamer *Arakaka*; reported by radio.

This was M. Bombard's curious craft, in which he made his survival experiments on a successful transatlantic passage in 1953. What vessel the other was I never discovered, nor did Lloyd's. It might have been Mrs Ann Davison's small *Felicity Ann,* except that her sloop was only twenty-three feet long.

Mrs Davison successfully sailed her yacht across the Atlantic. So have at least a hundred other people. Some of them almost make a business of it, or a way of life. Humphrey Barton, in his book *Atlantic Adventurers*, gives a list of 110 well-known Atlantic crossings by yacht up to that time, thirty-two of them single-handed, seventeen in boats not more than twenty feet long. Nor did the list include transatlantic races of which there have been many.

Not all these yachts have gone off for fun, or sport, or the love of sailing. Several have been manned by refugees usually from Baltic countries.

Baltic Refugees Sail Across Atlantic

Buenos Aires, Nov. 15, 1948

Two small sailing vessels, the *Elsa,* of 43 tons, and the *Olinda,* 27 tons, from the Baltic, have arrived in Buenos Aires roads unexpectedly, and without documents, bringing some 70 Finnish,

German, Latvian, Lithuanian, and Russian refugees. Although the newcomers have not complied with the Argentine immigration regulations, it is considered certain that the Argentine Government will show its traditional hospitality and allow them to settle in Argentine.

Lloyd's List

The escape of the *Elsa* and *Olinda* was not unique. A group of Estonians sailed a yacht named *Erma* from the Baltic to Norfolk, Virginia, in 1945, with sixteen men, women and children aboard, though the *Erma* was nothing but a small old sloop designed to provide accommodation for four. They were over four months at sea, but they made it.

Nor are all refugees confined to the North Atlantic—not by any means. Voyages enforced by island famines are no new idea in the Pacific Ocean or the East Indies. They still go on, like this one reported in the Australian Press.

450-Mile Voyage in a Canoe

Darwin, March 28, 1960

With only the sun and stars as guides, six natives have reached Australia in a dug-out canoe from the lonely island of Seroea, in the Banda Sea, about 450 miles north of Darwin. The canoe was stranded on a reef near Cape Don, 40 miles from Darwin. A naval launch brought the natives to Darwin, where they said that they had come to seek work. Because of their ignorance of the Australian immigration laws, the authorities may allow the natives to stay for a few weeks.

Local seamen consider the natives' feat with a 21-ft. canoe astonishing. The voyage took only 12 days, and the canoe arrived soon after a native sailing vessel with a crew of 19 had come from Seroea to seek food, because of famine on their island.

SINGLE-HANDED TRANSATLANTIC RACE

Ocean yacht races are nothing new. There are the great "classics"—the Fastnet Race (which would be quite a test of any sailing vessel), the Bermuda Race (with almost a hundred fine yachts in it in 1960), the Honolulu Race, the Sydney to Hobart Race in the South Pacific. Most of these are held biennially. Shorter races, just as tough, are conducted annually in the North Sea, the English Channel, Bay of Biscay, West Indies waters among others.

Such races are real and they are certainly earnest. Ocean racing is a sport for "tough guys"—the toughest of the tough.

But the toughest race of all was held in 1960—a *single-handed* race across the North Atlantic westwards, from Plymouth to New York. This race was organised by Lt.-Col. H. G. Haslar, not as a stunt but as a serious, gruelling test of small yachts—and that it was. Four yachts, each manned by one man, sailed from Plymouth in a fresh wind upon a June day in 1960. A fifth soon followed them. They were an odd assortment, the hard residue of an original 150 inquiries.

My favourite was Haslar himself, but the race was won by the oldest—and least experienced—man in it, with the most awkward and the largest yacht. This was the fifty-eight-year-old Francis Chichester, and his vessel was the twelve-ton *Gipsy Moth III*, some forty feet long and not most men's idea of a vessel suited for single-handed work.

Not only did Chichester win, but he sailed across in forty days—good going to the west'ard even for a big ship with all the crew she needed. Chichester's performance was remarkable.

He told reporters on his arrival at New York on July 22, 1960, he had been thirty-nine days without sighting land. Then on the Wednesday he saw Block Island off the tip of Long Island, just north of New York. "I clocked my 4,000th mile today—and it's only 3,000 miles from Plymouth to New York," he said. "As far as I was concerned it was 4,000 miles to windward. Every time I tried to get to New York there was the wind coming straight at me."

He admitted he had been lonely and sometimes afraid. "The Atlantic is always terrifying. You can't imagine how a boat can survive. That's one of the worst parts of a solo trip —the terrific pounding, pounding, pounding of the waves."

Mrs Chichester, at the same time, was reported as stating

that her husband had been given only a few weeks to live some time previously, and he took up yachting as part of his self-prescribed treatment to defy such pessimism. The race—she called it a "trip"—was also part of the treatment.

All of this, the wonderfully good performance of yacht and man, the scorn for a medical death sentence, and (perhaps even more rare) the humility and quiet behaviour on arrival—were in keeping with Chichester the man. I'd chanced to know him slightly, back in his flying days, when he was flying small single-engined biplanes over enormous distances towards difficult landfalls—always not only with success, but quiet success: no accidents, no promotion, no ballyhoo. That is Chichester. Forty days to New York in a forty-foot boat, single-handed! As a sailing performance, in its own way, it ranks with the clippers.

Nor was Haslar very far behind—only a few days, and his little ship was twenty-five feet long, with lots of gear of his own design being tried out the hard way, for the first time.

It was altogether a memorable achievement, in every way.

11—OSAM

WAR

WAR

IN the First World War I was in Australia—far off, then.
I saw the troopships go and the sailing-ships lie for weeks
at the anchorage in Port Philip Bay, loaded and ready for
sea but unable to sail for lack of crews. I would have
shipped in any of them gladly, and tried more than once.
Perhaps it was as well I did not, for many did not arrive.
Submarines, mines, raiders beat them up. The decimation
of the Cape Horn sailing-ship which then went on just
about killed off the breed. Only two big sailers were built
afterwards, both Germans, both Laeisz "P" four-masters.

At least the 1914–18 war produced one grand sea story,
in the shape of Count Felix von Luckner's extraordinary
cruise in the full-rigged ship *Pass of Balmaha*.

If the Second World War produced any such story, I
have yet to hear of it. At sea it was a grim and murderous
business, unrelieved by anything but the wonderful courage
of many who suffered in it—none more so than some quiet
merchant seamen trying to bring boats to safety after their
murdered ships had gone down.

Like Angus MacDonald, able seaman in the Ellerman
Line's *City of Cairo*, and the English girl who was with him
in the only surviving boat, whose story, *Ordeal*, is given in
this section.

FELIX COUNT VON LUCKNER

Felix Count von Luckner began a crowded life as a merchant
seaman. His exploit of taking an old full-rigged ship
through the otherwise effective British blockade in the
First World War, and turning into a highly successful and

benevolent pirate the while he cheerfully sank some 100,000 tons of much-needed Allied ships, remains—for me at any rate, and for a great many other people too—the *only* colourful, unbloody, and almost romantic achievement not only of the first but from both horrible world wars. The Count went to the greatest pains not only to save the lives of those whose ships he had to sink, but to make them all as comfortable as possible and to land them in some neutral port as soon as he could. His *Seeadler* (which I had known earlier as the Limejuice full-rigger *Pass of Balmaha*) was finally wrecked by natural forces in a lagoon called Mopelia among the delectable South Sea islands, and the Count became a prisoner briefly in New Zealand. His exploit was notable, and not only for its humanity.

Years afterwards, when he had a four-mast schooner called *Mopelia* lying alongside the 157th Street pier in the Hudson River at New York City and I was visiting port in the ship *Joseph Conrad*, I met the Count, and later spent many pleasant hours aboard his ship yarning with him. A great, jovial fellow with hands like hams and a Cape Horn voice, he spread his medals on the schooner's saloon table—boxes and boxes of them, which he displayed with the interest and delight of a first-voyage apprentice! This cross from the Pope, because he had spared so many lives, this other enamelled and glittering cross from some government which also had no part in the war but was moved by the same spirit as His Holiness. Crosses for valour, medals for Jutland, for action after action in war and peace. The vast array of crosses, medals and such clinked together on the table as he handled them, in the metallic, callous way that medals do, when wars are over.

There was the Count, brave and brilliant seaman, born diplomat, natural expert in good international relations, sitting there showing them, unemployed in a humdrum world and, in reality, regarded as unemployable. The *Mopelia* lay in New York for years. Apart from a sort of West Indies cruise organised by someone else, with college boys—too many college boys—I don't think she went again to sea at all, until she returned to Germany and was burned out in the Hamburg docks.

Others exploited the Count's achievements. There was a best-selling book and there was a "comic"-strip series. The Count was making a living giving wayside lectures, and ripping Manhattan telephone directories apart with those great ham hands. A world at "peace" had no place for a benevolent pirate, nor indeed for an outstanding sailing-ship master of proven initiative and enterprise.

During the Second World War, when again enterprising German long-voyage raiders broke the blockade and did far too much damage to Allied shipping, I put forward a scheme once to re-rig the former German four-masted barque *Peking*, then lying as the *Arethusa* in the River Medway near the naval base of Chatham. My idea was to use her as a sort of Q-ship against these German raiders. I thought the Count might be among their number again and, even if he were not, any German naval reserve officer aboard might be interested in a "P" ship, war or no war. There were still a couple such German ships which the *Peking* could have passed as—her sister-ship *Priwall*, for one. If the Count or any of his compatriots ventured close enough, an underwater torpedo or two would put paid to them. It would, I thought, be one against my friend the Count which he would be the first to appreciate. But he was not in any such ship. One or two of the raider captains of '39–45 might have fallen but, on the whole, they were seamen of a different mould. In any event, My Lords of the Admiralty turned the idea down, perhaps wisely.

In the chapter on the *Seeadler*, the Official British History of the Great War reveals what the British Admiralty officially thought of the old "windjammer" which had caused them many headaches.

The new raider was the *Seeadler*, formerly the ship *Pass of Balmaha*: and her captain, Count von Luckner. . . . His story claims our attention for the thoroughness and skill with which he had prepared his cruise, and our admiration for the seamanlike chivalry with which he conducted it. . . . In all the testimonies of his English and French prisoners there is no word of complaint against him; some men go out of their way to say that he treated them kindly; we can therefore conclude, with certainty, that he was a bold, calculating and adventurous leader; and we have every reason to believe that he was a kindly and courteous gentleman as well. . . .

On March 21 he seized the French sailing-ship *Cambronne,* which was carrying Chilean nitrates to France, and to her he transferred all his prisoners. . . .

The prisoners and their captor parted on extremely good terms. Count von Luckner had taken no precautions against the *Seeadler* being captured by them; thinking probably that their difference of race and language made all concerted action between them impossible. Everybody had, therefore, been allowed to roam about the ship as he wished; and apart from this, Count von Luckner had several times acted graciously and generously. . . . All this had impressed the prisoners, as well it might; so that they were transferred to the *Cambronne* with cheers and shouting; and even the French masters, whose proud, implacable attitude had deeply impressed Count von Luckner, shook hands with him before they went over the side for the last time.

SIR HENRY NEWBOLT: *Naval Operations,* volume IV of the History of the Great War, based on official documents.

The Cape Horning old Count writes cheerfully of his first visit to London after the First World War, in 1935. He was fêted and invited everywhere.

One invitation I accepted with particular delight; it was from a group of naval officers who included a number who had spent a great deal of their time during the war chasing me and my *Seeadler.* I now went to see them as their guest on board a battleship which happened to be lying in harbour.

Long tables festively decorated were set out on the quarterdeck under awnings, and there stood my hosts and one-time enemies awaiting my arrival. The first to greet me with outstetched hand was Admiral Sir Aubrey Smith. As commander of the *Glasgow* he had been the nightmare of all German auxiliary cruisers. He was the one who was always close on our tails and all of us knew him by name. It was he who now made a speech of welcome to me, one of those he had formerly hunted.

"At last one of our heartfelt wishes has now been granted," he began. "If a little late. We have come face to face with a man we would have liked very much to come face to face with somewhat earlier. We chased him through the seven seas, but we

The full-rigged ship *Grace Harwar* was the last such ship in the Cape Horn grain trade—a beauty, but a killer. I took the photograph from one of her boats in the south-east trade winds while homeward-bound from Wallaroo in 1929. She had then a crew of 13 hands before the mast, but killed one of them on the road to Cape Horn. Here she is under all sail

Sailor's eye-view from aloft, looking down from the main on the bows of the *Grace Harwar* in a day of fresh trade winds. The foam rolls wide before the bows, the wind-distended foresail curves beautifully at its work of pulling the old ship on. Every sail swells with its effort. The main deck is dry, the weather good, the sailors cheerful, for the ship is running a nice 12 knots. She is loaded with 3000 tons of South Australian grain, was 138 days from Wallaroo to Queenstown for orders. I got the picture from the main lower topgallant yard

Louis S. Martel

Aboard such a ship Herman Melville sailed—the American whaler *Charles W. Morgan* in her permanent berth at the Mystic Marine Museum, Mystic, Connecticut, U.S.A. The *Morgan* was built in 1841, is reputed to have taken whalebone and oil worth $2,000,000 in some 75 years of whaling voyages

Figurehead of the ship *Balclutha* stares beneath the old Scots full-rigger's long bowsprit in shipyard at San Francisco where the 70-year-old ship was restored and rerigged. The *Balclutha* lies permanently preserved near the Fishermen's Dock in San Francisco today. In such ships Masefield, Conrad, Bone saw service, and James Learmont commanded. The *Balclutha* was first an ordinary Scots tramp. Later she sailed out of San Francisco in the Alaska salmon-packing trade, as the *Star of Alaska*

Furling the Crojack—a good stow. Watch of the *Parma* aloft
furling the weather side of the lowest sail on the mizzen-mast.
Wire footrope supports them, steel jackstay along the top of the
yard gives them a grip. Most of these sailors are cadets, average
age 17 to 18. They do not look down, only at their work,
adjusting themselves without thought to the ship's motion

When the long-voyage sailing-ships approached the Trade winds, all sails were changed. Hot sun and Doldrums rain were hard on canvas: any old sails served that part of the voyage. Here aboard the *Parma* young seamen prepare to change the fore lower topsail. The best sail, now bent, is clewed up and unbent. Then an older sail is hauled aloft and bent in its place. Sailors delighted in such work

Fox Photos

The working Thames barge, for hundreds of years the "roust-about" of the London River, now gone. Handy, weatherly, able, the barge did splendidly the work for which she was evolved—cheap distributive haulage for the port and estuary—but the motor-lorry and powered barges spelled her end. A man and a boy could handle her, for her gear was astonishingly simple to use. A few barges have made ocean passages. Once three sailed to Rio de Janeiro

Planet News

A handful for one man—Francis Chichester sailed his sloop *Gipsy Moth III* single-handed to the westward across the North Atlantic in 40 days, winning the first-ever single-handed ocean race. Small sail aft is self-steering gear, designed to shift the rudder when the sloop tries to get off course. Chichester—a former airman distinguished for outstanding solo flights—waves from the afterdeck as he wins never managed to catch up with him. Well, here he is now, an honoured guest on the deck of a British warship."

Amongst the officers gathered there was one I had every reason to recognize: Captain Holland. He had once spent two hours searching my ship, and in the end he had let me go, wishing me "Good luck", on the way.

Admiral Smith turned to him:

"Well, Holland, eighteen years ago you stood on the deck of Count Luckner's ship, and her fate and his were in your hands. For two hours you searched his camouflaged sailing-ship and questioned her captain. And then you let him go, benevolently wishing him a safe voyage. No less benevolently he then proceeded to sink shipping to the value of five million pounds sterling. Today you are again with him. Are you sorry you let him go?"

At that Captain Holland sprang to his feet and exclaimed: "From all accounts, sir, and that includes even our own official history, it is quite clear that the operations of the *Seeadler* represented the only really romantic episode of the war at sea; a man showed that you could do big things with an old windjammer even in modern scientific warfare. With his sailing-ship Count Luckner waged a gentleman's war against us. Looked at rightly, sir, you have to thank me for the only romantic episode in modern sea warfare. If I hadn't let Count Luckner and his ship go, naval history would have been the poorer."

And at these words all the officers sprang to their feet and cheered to the echo.

"Three cheers for the last of the pirates!" someone shouted, and they were given with a will.

COUNT FELIX VON LUCKNER: *Out of an Old Sea Chest*

Basil Lubbock, the well-known sailing-ship historian, gives the *Seeadler* story in some detail in recounting the history of the old *Pass of Balmaha*. She was quite a fast ship.

"Pass of Balmaha" as a German Raider

The 1,500-ton steel full-rigger *Pass of Balmaha* was built by Duncan for Gibson and Clark of Glasgow: she was Duncan's 237th, and though like every other builder at this date he had to consider carrying capacity before sailing qualities, he managed to give the *Pass of Balmaha* a good turn of speed for a full-built ship. But she will be remembered rather as the German raider

Seeadler (Sea Eagle) during the Great War, when she was so ably commanded by the daring Graf Felix von Luckner, who sank millions of pounds worth of French and British shipping, including, alas, some fine square-riggers.

Some of her sailing performances in her early days are worthy of record. In 1899, under Captain Scougall, she went from Newcastle, N.S.W. to Sourabaya in 42 days. Then in 1900 Captain Scougall sailed from Buenos Ayres to Newcastle, N.S.W. in 42 days. The *Pass of Balmaha* had strong westerly winds as far as Bass Straits, where a head wind induced her master to bear away south to round the Island when he got a fair wind again. The *Pass of Balmaha*'s average was 236 miles per day, her best run being 336 miles.

In 1901 the ship arrived off the Isle of Wight, 103 days out from New Caledonia.

In 1901 the *Pass of Balmaha* broke the record between the River Plate and Boston, making this run in 34 days.

She had just been sold by Gibson and Clark to the River Plate Shipping Company, and was commanded at the time by Captain Dick Lee, a very fine example of Blue-nose shipmaster.

When war broke out she was commanded by a New England skipper named Scott, and was on a passage from New York to Archangel under the American flag when a suspicious British cruiser held her up and sent her to Scapa Flow under a prize officer and six men. Then whilst she was on her way a German submarine popped up and took the old ship, prize crew and all, into Cuxhaven.

After the battle of Jutland the German Naval authorities realised that there was little hope of their cruisers being able to avoid the enemy on the high seas, and decided that camouflaged merchantmen were their only chance as commerce destroyers outside the radius of their submarines. The *Pass of Balmaha* was a very clever choice for their desperate object, as none of the allied cruisers were likely to suspect a windjammer of being a German warship. Luckily for the success of the enterprise, there happened to be a German naval officer who was perfectly suited for the command of such a vessel. This was Commander Graf Felix von Luckner, who had commanded cruisers at the battles of Heligoland and Jutland; at Jutland his vessel had been sunk and he was picked out of the sea severely wounded. The Count, however, was a tough customer; not only was he a champion swimmer, but he held the German record for saving life from drowning, so that it is not surprising that he managed to keep afloat until he was rescued, in spite of being badly wounded. His chief hobby was yachting, and he was a devotee of the out-of-date square-rigged sailing-ship, having not only served in the past for a year as A.B. on a Norwegian windjammer, but also in the fo'c'sle of the British four-mast barque, *Pinmore*.

The Germans were as thorough as even they could be in the preparation of the *Seeadler*, as the *Pass of Balmaha* was re-named; everything was thought out down to the tiniest detail.

First of all, the ship was fitted with an auxiliary engine of 1,500 horse-power; besides two four-point-twos, machine guns, carbines, bombs and a powerful wireless plant all were concealed behind secret doors; hidden accommodation being even prepared for future prisoners.

Next came the selection and training of the crew. To the number of 64, they were all picked men from the Naval Reserve, most of whom had served in the merchant ships of many nationalities besides their own. Although von Luckner, his navigating officer and most of his crew could speak Norwegian, this in itself was not considered sufficient to disguise the raider into an innocent Norwegian trader.

For several weeks before sailing the crew were trained in Norwegian ways and methods of carrying on at sea. All orders were given in that language, and the Count himself was so thorough in playing his part that he grew a beard and learnt to chew tobacco and spit brown. All naval discipline and habits were strictly tabooed, for fear of the keen eyes of the British naval officer.

As soon as von Luckner was satisfied that his deck hands would pass as Norwegians and that his gun crews were efficient, the *Seeadler*, as we will now call her, took on board a deck cargo of very heavy timber, which effectually blocked all entry to the hold, except by secret doors. Next sufficient provisions were taken in for a three years' cruise. Perhaps the most important and skilfully contrived deception of the lot were the ship's papers. These showed that the *Seeadler* was the Norwegian ship *Irma*, bound out to Melbourne, to which the rubber stamp of the British Consulate bore witness.

The *Seeadler*, ex *Pass of Balmaha*, left German waters for the high seas on December 21, 1916, and such bad weather was experienced in rounding the Scottish coast that no enemy ship was sighted. However, at 9.30 a.m. on Christmas Day, when about 180 miles south of Iceland, the new raider sighted the British cruiser *Highland Scot*. First a blank and then a shotted charge was fired at the innocent looking full-rig ship, which had all sail set to a light breeze. Captain von Luckner, having gained sufficient time to make his preparations, now hove to, whilst the cruiser circled round with every gun trained in his direction. Having had a good look at the strange sailing-ship, the *Highland Scot* now hauled off a few lengths and sent a boat to examine the *Seeadler*.

Von Luckner's plans for just such an emergency were complete. Only five men, all of whom could speak Norwegian, showed themselves on the deck of the raider, besides her captain, who, as the boat came alongside, could be heard bellowing orders in Norwegian whilst his men lowered a rope ladder over the side.

Two officers and an armed party of 12 bluejackets came over the rail to be properly hoodwinked by the daring Count, who almost overplayed his part in his zeal as an actor.

After greeting the boarding officer with "A Happy Christmas to you", he took him aft to his cabin in order to show the ship's papers. I will give what followed in his own words:*

"In the saloon, lying on a divan, I had a seventeen-year-old boy, dressed as a woman and possessing a very clear complexion and feminine appearance. He was carefully dressed for the part he had to play, and a shawl was wrapped round his head as if he were suffering from toothache.

"I introduced this specimen of human camouflage to the officer as my wife, who was 'very sick'. Whereupon he said, 'I hope you will excuse me, lady, I am only doing my duty, and will only be here for a short time in which to look at the ship's papers.' There was only one danger regarding the boy's make-up, and that was his voice, which might have betrayed him by reason of its roughness. Fortunately the suppositious 'toothache' excused him from talking. Part of my cabin fittings were Norwegian cushion covers, and on the walls were displayed photos of Norway's King and Queen, also a photo of King Edward VII.

"While the officer was proceeding with the examination of my papers a gramophone in the mess-room was playing 'It's a Long Way to Tipperary', whilst several of the examining officer's men were taken to the pantry, where the steward supplied them with a glass of good whisky, which made everyone cheerful and created a good impression.

"During this time I was chewing tobacco and expectorating on the floor, after the manner of a Norwegian captain."

* Quoted from Von Luckner's own pamphlet on his exploits, written while a prisoner-of-war in New Zealand and published in August 1919.

(I fancy that Norwegian captains will accuse him of overplaying his part here.)

"When the examination was finished, the officer shook hands with me and said, 'Captain, your papers are all right, but you must wait until you get the order by signal to continue your voyage.' I thereupon assumed an anxious look and asked if I would be safe from submarines, and could he give me any advice. He replied: 'I don't think you will find any so far North as we now are.'

"The officer and his crew then left my ship and went aboard the cruiser, and in about half an hour the signal, 'Continue your voyage', was hoisted. Oh, what a relief was felt by everyone on board when that signal was given. After this the cruiser passed us once more. We gave her three cheers and dipped our Norwegian flag. She then showed another signal 'Happy Voyage', to which I replied 'Thank you very much'. 'That is just what I want,' said I to my chief officer, and felt indeed a happy man."

BASIL LUBBOCK: Last of the Windjammers

I sometimes wondered what might have happened if, instead of being allowed to proceed by a cruiser, the Count had instead been intercepted by a sailing-ship sailor aboard one of our British Q-ships of the time. Several of them were small sailing-ships. Conrad served in one. I don't think, somehow, that the *Irma* would have fooled him.

JOHN PAUL JONES

Whoever or whatever the enigmatic John Paul "Jones" may have been, he was a splendid fighter. Born John Paul in Scotland, calling himself Jones for reasons of his own in America, as a former merchant seaman he became one of the few commanders who got to sea for his new country during the Wars of the American Revolution. He did well, but nobody appears to have liked him—not his own officers, nor any other captains required to work under his orders. Benjamin Franklin, at the time American Minister in Paris, did see his qualities, and obtained him command of a decrepit old French East Indiaman which Jones renamed

173

Bon homme Richard. With this seagoing wreck, disorganised and poorly manned, Jones took on the new English 44-gun *Serapis*, which should have been able to blow him out of the sea. Here he reports to Benjamin Franklin just what happened—quite a story.

On board the ship *Serapis*, at anchor, October 3, 1779, His Excellency Benjamin Franklin:
... About noon we saw and chased a large ship that appeared coming round Flamborough Head from the northward. Soon after this a fleet of 41 sail appeared off Flamborough Head, bearing N.N.E. When the fleet discovered us bearing down, all the merchant ships crowded sail towards the shore. The two ships of war that protected the fleet at the same time steered from the land, and made the disposition for the battle. In approaching the enemy, I crowded every possible sail, and made the signal for the line of battle, to which the *Alliance* showed no attention. Earnest as I was for the action, I could not reach the commodore's ship until seven in the evening. Being then within pistol shot, when he hailed the *Bon homme Richard*, we answered him by firing a whole broadside.

The battle, being thus begun, was continued with unremitting fury. Every method was practised on both sides to gain an advantage, and rake each other; and I must confess that the enemy's ship, being much more manageable than the *Bon homme Richard*, gained thereby several times an advantageous situation, in spite of my best endeavours to prevent it. As I had to deal with an enemy of *greatly superior force*, I was under the necessity of closing with him, to prevent the advantage which he had over me in point of manoeuvre. It was my intention to lay the *Bon homme Richard* athwart the enemy's bow; but, as that operation required great dexterity in the management of both sails and helm, and some of our braces being shot away, it did not exactly succeed to my wishes. The enemy's bowsprit, however, came over the *Bon homme Richard*'s poop by the mizzen mast, and I made both ships fast together in that situation, which by the action of the wind on the enemy's sails forced her stern close to the *Bon homme Richard*'s bow, so that the ships lay square alongside of each other, the yards being all entangled, and the cannon of each ship touching the opponent's side.

When this position took place, it was 8 o'clock, previous to which the *Bon homme Richard* had received sundry eighteen-pounds shot below the water, and leaked very much. My battery of

12-pounders, on which I had placed my chief dependence, being commanded by Lieut. Dale and Col. Weibert, and manned principally with American seamen and French volunteers, were entirely silenced and abandoned. As to the six old eighteen-pounders that formed the battery of the lower gun-deck, they did no service whatever. Two out of three of them burst at the first fire, and killed almost all the men who were stationed to manage them. Before this time, too, Col. de Chamillard, who commanded a party of 20 soldiers on the poop, had abandoned that station after having lost some of his men. These men deserted their quarters. I had now only two pieces of cannon, nine-pounders, on the quarter-deck, that were not silenced; and not one of the heavier cannon was fired during the rest of the action. The purser, Mr Mease, who commanded the guns on the quarter deck, being dangerously wounded in the head, I was obliged to fill his place, and with great difficulty rallied a few men, and shifted over one of the lee quarter-deck guns, so that we afterward played three pieces of 9-pounders upon the enemy. The tops alone seconded the fire of this little battery, and held out bravely during the whole of the action, especially the main top, where Lieut. Stack commanded. I directed the fire of one of the three cannon against the main-mast, with double-headed shot, while the other two were exceedingly well served with grape and canister shot to silence the enemy's musketry, and clear her decks, which was at last effected.

The enemy were, as I have since understood, on the instant of calling for quarters when the cowardice or treachery of three of my under officers induced them to call to the enemy. The English commodore asked me if I demanded quarters; and, I having answered him in the most determined negative, they renewed the battle with double fury. They were unable to stand the deck; but the fire of their cannon, especially the lower battery, which was entirely formed of 18-pounders, was incessant. Both ships were set on fire in various places, and the scene was dreadful beyond the reach of language. To account for the timidity of my three under officers—I mean the gunner, the carpenter, and the master-at-arms—I must observe that the two first were slightly wounded; and, as the ship had received various shots under water, and one of the pumps being shot away, the carpenter expressed his fear that she would sink, and the other two concluded that she was sinking, which occasioned the gunner to run aft on the poop without my knowledge to strike the colors. Fortunately for me, a cannon ball had done that before by carrying away the ensign staff. He was therefore reduced to the necessity of sinking, as he supposed, or of calling for quarter; and he preferred the latter.

All this time the *Bon homme Richard* had sustained the action alone, and the enemy, though much superior in force, would have been very glad to have got clear, as appears by their own acknowledgements, and by their having let go an anchor the instant that I laid them on board, by which means they would have escaped, had I not made them well fast to the *Bon homme Richard*.

At last, at half-past 9 o'clock, the *Alliance* appeared, and I now thought the battle at an end; but, to my utter astonishment, he discharged a broadside full into the stern of the *Bon homme Richard*. We called to him for God's sake to forbear firing into the *Bon homme Richard*; yet he passed along the off side of the ship, and continued firing. There was no possibility of his mistaking the enemy's ship for the *Bon homme Richard,* there being the most essential difference in their appearance and construction; besides, it was then full moonlight, and the sides of the *Bon homme Richard* were all black, while the sides of the prizes were yellow; yet, for the greater security, I shewed the signal of our reconnoissance by putting out three lanthorns, one at the head (bow), another at the stern (quarter), and the third in the middle in a horizontal line. Every tongue cried that he was firing into the wrong ship, but nothing availed. He passed round, firing into the *Bon homme Richard's* head, stern, and broadside; and by one of his volleys killed several of my best men, and mortally wounded a good officer on the forecastle. My situation was really deplorable. The *Bon homme Richard* received various shots under water from the *Alliance,* the leak gained on the pumps, and the fire increased much on board both ships. Some officers persuaded me to strike, of whose courage and good sense I entertain a high opinion. My treacherous master-at-arms let loose all my prisoners without my knowledge, and my prospect became gloomy indeed. I would not, however, give up the point. The enemy's main-mast began to shake, their firing decreased, ours rather increased, and the British colors were struck at half an hour past 10 o'clock.

This prize proved to be the British ship of war, the *Serapis,* a new ship of 44 guns, built on their most approved construction, with two complete batteries, one of them of 18-pounders, and commanded by the brave Commodore Richard Pearson. I had yet two enemies to encounter far more formidable than the Britons—I mean fire and water. The *Serapis* was attacked only by the first, but the *Bon homme Richard* was assailed by both. There were five feet of water in the hold, and, though it was moderate from the explosion of so much gunpowder, yet the three pumps that remained could with difficulty only keep the water from gaining. The fire broke out in various parts of the ship, in spite of all the water that could be thrown to quench it, and at length broke out as low as the powder magazine, and within a few inches of the powder. In that dilemma I took out the powder upon deck, ready to be thrown overboard at the last extremity; and it was ten o'clock the next day, the 24th, before the fire was entirely extinguished. With respect to the situation of the *Bon homme Richard,* the rudder was cut entirely off the stern frame, and the transoms were almost entirely cut away; the timbers, by the lower deck especially, from the mainmast to the stern, being greatly decayed with age, were mangled beyond my power of description; and a person must have been an eye-witness to form a just idea of the tremendous scene of carnage, wreck, and ruin that every-where appeared. Humanity cannot but recoil from the prospect of such finished horror, and lament that war should produce such fatal consequences.

After the carpenters, as well as Capt. de Cottineau, and other men of sense, had well examined and surveyed the ship (which was not finished before five in the evening), I found every person to be convinced that it was impossible to keep the *Bon homme Richard* afloat so as to reach a port if the wind should increase, it being then only a very moderate breeze. I had but little time to remove my wounded, which now became unavoidable, and which was effected in the course of the night and the next morning. I was determined to keep the *Bon homme Richard* afloat, and, if possible, to bring her into port. For that purpose the first lieutenant of the *Pallas* continued on board with a party of men to attend the pumps, with boats in waiting ready to take them on board in case the water should gain on them too fast. The wind augmented in the night and the next day, on the 25th, so that it was impossible to prevent the good old ship from sinking. They did not abandon her till after 9 o'clock. The water was then up to the lower deck, and a little after ten I saw with inexpressible grief the last glimpse of the *Bon homme Richard.* No lives were lost with the ship, but it was impossible to save the stores of any sort whatever. I lost even the best part of my clothes, books, and papers; and several of my officers lost all their clothes and effects.

Captain Cottineau engaged the *Countess of Scarborough,* and

177

took her after an hour's action, while the *Bon homme Richard* engaged the *Serapis*. The *Countess of Scarborough* is an armed ship of 20 six-pounders, and was commanded by a king's officer. In the action the *Countess of Scarborough* and the *Serapis* were at a considerable distance asunder; and the *Alliance*, as I am informed, fired into the *Pallas*, and killed some men. If it should be asked why the convoy was suffered to escape, I must answer that I was myself in no condition to pursue, and that none of the rest showed any inclination. The *Alliance*, too, was in a state to pursue the fleet, not having had a single man wounded or a single shot fired at her from the *Serapis*. and only three that did execution from the *Countess of Scarborough*, at such a distance that one stuck in the side, and the other two just touched and then dropped into the water. The *Alliance* killed one man only on board the *Serapis*.

As Captain de Cottineau charged himself with manning and securing the prisoners of the *Countess of Scarborough*, I think the escape of the Baltic fleet cannot so well be charged to his account.

I should have mentioned that the main-mast and mizzen-top-mast of the *Serapis* fell overboard soon after the captain had come on board the *Bon homme Richard*. . . .

Having thus endeavored to give a clear and simple relation of the circumstances and events that have attended the little armament under my command, I shall freely submit my conduct therein to the censure of my superiors and the impartial public. I beg leave, however, to observe that the force that was put under my command was far from being well composed; and, as the great majority of the actors in it have appeared bent on the pursuit of interest only . . .

I am ever, etc.,

JOHN P. JONES

When it comes to sailing-ships, we have a pretty long tradition of heroic endeavours in our own history—none more stirring than the last fight of Sir Richard Grenville's little *Revenge*.

"At Flores in the Azores Sir Richard Grenville lay."

How often had Tennyson's opening line conjured up visions for me, back at school! "Flores in the Azores"— there is a wonderful ring just in that. Fifty-three enemy ships lie off the port. The seamen are surprised.

> "Shall we fight or shall we fly?
>   Good Sir Richard, tell us now;
>   For to fight is but to die.
> There'll be little of us left by the time this sun is set."
>   And Sir Richard said again: "We be all good Englishmen;
>   Let us bang these dogs of Seville, the children of the devil,
>   For I never turned my back on don or devil yet."

So they got on with the battle, one against the fifty-three.

The Hakluyt Society gives the story factually, in cold prose: but the grandeur and the moving inspiration of it leap out from the lines.

Action off the Azores, 1591

The Lord Thomas Howard with six of Her Majesty's ships, six victuallers of London, the bark *Raleigh,* and two or three other pinnaces riding at anchor near unto Flores, one of the westerly islands of the Azores, the last of August in the afternoon, had intelligence by one Captain Middleton of the approach of the Spanish Armada. Which Middleton, being in a very good sailer, had kept them company three days before, of good purpose, both to discover their forces the more, as also to give advice to my Lord Thomas of their approach. He had no sooner delivered the news but the fleet was in sight: many of our ships' companies were on shore in the island, some providing ballast for their ships, others filling of water and refreshing themselves from the land with such things as they could either for money or by force recover. By reason whereof our ships being all pestered and rummaging everything out of order, very light for want of ballast, and that which was most to our disadvantage, the one-half part of the men of every ship sick, and utterly unserviceable; for in the *Revenge* there were ninety diseased, in the *Bonaventure* not so many in health as could handle her mainsail.

The Spanish fleet having shrouded their approach by reason of the island, were now so soon at hand, as our ships had scarce time to weigh their anchors, but some of them were driven to let slip their cables and set sail. Sir Richard Grenville was the last that weighed, to recover the men that were upon the island, which otherwise had been lost. The Lord Thomas with the rest very hardly recovered the wind, which Sir Richard Grenville, not being able to do, was persuaded by the master and others to cut his main-sail and cast about, and to trust to the sailing of the ship, for the squadron of Seville were on his weather-bow. But Sir Richard utterly refused to turn from the enemy, alleging that he would rather choose to die, than to dishonour himself, his country, and Her Majesty's ships, persuading his company that he would pass through the two squadrons in despite of them, and enforce those of Seville to give him way. Which he performed upon divers of the foremost, who, as the mariners term it, sprang their luff, and fell under the lee of the *Revenge*. But the other course had been the better and might right well have been answered in so great an impossibility of prevailing. Notwithstanding, out of the greatness of his mind he could not be persuaded. In the meanwhile, as he attended those which were nearest him, the great *San Philip* being in the wind of him, and coming towards him, becalmed his sails in such sort as the ship could neither make way nor feel her helm, so huge and high carged was the Spanish ship, being of a thousand and five hundred tons. Who often laid the *Revenge* aboard. When he was thus bereft of his sails, the ships that were under his lee luffing up also laid him aboard; of which the next was the *Admiral of the Biscayans*, a very mighty and puissant ship commanded by Brittandona. The said *Philip* carried three tier of ordnance on a side, and eleven pieces in every tier. She shot eight forth right of her chase, besides those of her stern ports.

After the *Revenge* was entangled with this *Philip*, four others boarded her; two on her larboard, and two on her starboard. The fight thus beginning at three of the clock in the afternoon continued very terrible all that evening. But the great *San Philip*, having received the lower tier of the *Revenge*, discharged with cross-bar shot, shifted herself with all diligence from her sides, utterly misliking her first entertainment. Some say that the ship foundered, but we cannot report it for truth unless we were assured. The Spanish ships were filled with companies of soldiers, in some two hundred, besides the mariners; in some five, in others eight hundred. In ours there were none at all, beside the mariners, but the servants of the commanders and some few voluntary gentlemen only. After many interchanged volleys of great ordnance and small shot, the Spaniards deliberated to enter the *Revenge*, and made divers attempts, hoping to force her by the multitudes of their armed soldiers and musketeers, but were still repulsed again and again, and at all times beaten back into their own ships, or into the seas. In the beginning of the fight, the *George Noble* of London, having received some shot through her by the Armadas, fell under the lee of the *Revenge,* asked Sir Richard what he would command him, being but one of the victuallers and of small force. Sir Richard bid him save himself, and leave him to his fortune. After the fight had thus, without intermission, continued while the day lasted and some hours of the night, many of our men were slain and hurt, and one of the great galleons of the armada and the admiral of the hulks both sunk, and in many other of the Spanish ships great slaughter was made. Some write that Sir Richard was very dangerously hurt almost at the beginning of the fight, and lay speechless for a time ere he recovered. But two of the *Revenge*'s own company, brought home in a ship of the line from the islands, examined by some of the lords and others affirmed that he was never so wounded as that he forsook the upper deck till an hour before midnight, and then being shot into the body with a musket, as he was a-dressing was again shot into the head, and withal his chirurgeon wounded to death.

But to return to the fight. The Spanish ships which attempted to board the *Revenge,* as they were wounded and beaten off, so always others came in their places, she having never less than two mighty galleons by her sides and aboard her, so that ere the morning, from three of the clock the day before, there had fifteen several armadas assailed her, and all so ill-approved their entertainment, as they were by the break of the day far more willing to hearken to a composition than hastily to make any more assaults or entries. But as the day increased, so our men decreased; and as the light grew more and more, so by so much more grew our discomforts. For none appeared in sight but enemies, saving one small ship called the *Pilgrim,* commanded by Jacob Whiddon, who hovered all night to see the success; but in the morning, bearing with the *Revenge,* was hunted like a hare amongst many ravenous hounds, but escaped.

All the powder of the *Revenge,* to the last barrel, was now spent, all her pikes broken, forty of her best men slain, and the most part of the rest hurt. In the beginning of the fight she had but one hundred free from sickness, and fourscore-and-ten sick, laid in hold upon the ballast—a small troop to man such a ship, and a weak garrison to resist so mighty an army. By those hundred all was sustained—the volleys, boardings and enterings of fifteen ships of war, besides those which beat her at large; on the contrary, the Spanish were always supplied with soldiers brought from every squadron; all manner of arms and powder at will. Unto ours there remained no comfort at all, no hope, no supply either of ships, men, or weapons; the masts all beaten overboard, all her tackle cut asunder, her upper work altogether rased, and in effect evened she was with the water, but the very foundation or bottom of a ship, nothing being left overhead either for flight or defence. Sir Richard, finding himself in this distress, and unable any longer to make resistance, having endured in this fifteen hours' fight the assault of fifteen several armadas all by turns aboard him, and by estimation eight hundred shot of great artillery, besides many assaults and entries, and that himself and the ship must needs be possessed by the enemy, who were now all cast in a ring round about him (the *Revenge* not able to move one way or other, but as she was moved with the waves and billow of the sea), commanded the master-gunner, whom he knew to be a most resolute man, to split and sink the ship, that thereby nothing might remain of glory or victory to the Spaniards, seeing in so many hours' fight and with so great a navy they were not able to take her, having had fifteen hours' time, about ten thousand men, and fifty and three sail of men-of-war to perform it withal, and persuaded the company, or as many as he could induce, to yield themselves unto God, and to the mercy of none else; but as they had, like valiant resolute men, repulsed so many enemies, they should not now shorten the honour of their nation by prolonging their own lives for a few hours or a few days.

There were slain and drowned in this fight well near one thousand of the enemies, and two special commanders, Don Luis de Sant John and Don George de Prunaria de Malaga, as the Spanish captain confesseth, besides divers others of special account, whereof as yet report is not made.

The admiral of the hulks and the *Ascension* of Seville were both sunk by the side of the *Revenge*; one other recovered the road of San Michael, and sunk also there; a fourth ran herself with the shore to save her men. Sir Richard died, as it is said, the second or third day aboard the *General*, and was by them greatly bewailed. What became of his body, whether it was buried in the sea or on the land we know not; the comfort that remaineth to his friends is that he hath ended his life honourably in respect of the reputation won to his nation and country, and of the same to his posterity, and that being dead he hath not outlived his own honour.

The following is the account which John Huighen van Linschoten, who was in the Azores at the time, gives of the death of Grenville:

Don Alonso himself would neither see him nor speak with him: all the rest of the captains and gentlemen went to visit him, and to comfort him in his hard fortune, wondering at his courage and stout heart for that he shewed not any sign of faintness nor changing of colour; but feeling the hour of death approach, he spake these words in Spanish and said,—'Here die I, Richard Grenville, with a joyful and quiet mind, for that I have ended my life as a true soldier ought to do, that hath fought for his country, Queen, religion, and honour, whereby my soul most joyful departeth out of this body, and shall always leave behind it an everlasting fame of a valiant and true soldier, that hath done his duty as he was bound to do.' When he had finished these, or such other like words, he gave up the ghost, with great and stout courage, and no man could perceive any sign of heaviness on him.

Melville on Lord Nelson

Very likely it is no new remark that the inventions of our time have at least brought about a change in sea-warfare in degree corresponding to the revolution in all warfare effected by the original introduction from China into Europe of gunpowder. The first European fire-arm, a clumsy contrivance, was, as is well known, scouted by no few of the knights as a base implement, good enough peradventure for weavers too craven to stand up crossing steel with steel in frank fight. But as ashore knightly valour, tho' shorn of its blazonry, did not cease with the knights, neither on the seas, though nowadays in encounters there a certain kind of displayed gallantry be fallen out of date as hardly applicable under changed circumstances, did the nobler qualities of such naval magnates as Don John of Austria, Doria, Van Tromp, Jean Bart, the long line of British Admirals and the American Decaturs of 1812 become obsolete with their wooden walls.

Nevertheless, to anybody who can hold the Present at its worth without being inappreciative of the Past, it may be forgiven, if to such an one the solitary old hulk at Portsmouth Nelson's *Victory*, seems to float there, not alone as the decaying monument of a fame incorruptible, but also as a poetic reproach, softened by its picturesqueness, to the *Monitors* and yet mightier hulls of the European ironclads. And this not altogether because such craft are unsightly, unavoidably lacking the symmetry and grand lines of the old battle-ships, but equally for other reasons.

There are some, perhaps, who while not altogether inaccessible to that poetic reproach just alluded to, may yet on behalf of the new order, be disposed to parry it; and this to the extent of iconoclasm, if need be. For example, prompted by the sight of the star inserted in the *Victory*'s quarter-deck designating the spot where the Great Sailor fell, these martial utilitarians may suggest considerations implying that Nelson's ornate publication of his person in battle was not only unnecessary, but not military, nay, savoured of foolhardiness and vanity. They may add, too, that at Trafalgar it was in effect nothing less than a challenge to death; and death came; and that but for his bravado the victorious Admiral might possibly have survived the battle; and so, instead of having his sagacious dying injunctions overruled by his immediate successor in command, he himself, when the contest was decided, might have brought his shattered fleet to anchor, a proceeding which might have averted the deplorable loss of life by shipwreck in the elemental tempest that followed the martial one.

Well, should we set aside the more disputable point whether for various reasons it was possible to anchor the fleet, then plausibly enough the Benthamites of war may urge the above.

But the *might-have-been* is but boggy ground to build on. And, certainly, in foresight as to the larger issue of an encounter, and anxious preparations for it—buoying the deadly way and mapping it out, as at Copenhagen—few commanders have been so painstakingly circumspect as this same reckless declarer of his person in fight.

Personal prudence even when dictated by quite other than selfish considerations surely is no special virtue in a military man; while an excessive love of glory, impassioning a less burning impulse, the honest sense of duty, is the first. If the name *Wellington* is not so much of a trumpet to the blood as the simpler name *Nelson*, the reason for this may perhaps be inferred from the above. Alfred in his funeral ode on the victor of Waterloo ventures not to call him the greatest soldier of all time, tho' in the same ode he invokes Nelson as "the greatest sailor since the world began".

At Trafalgar Nelson, on the brink of opening the fight, sat down and wrote his last brief will and testament. If under the presentiment of the most magnificent of all victories to be crowned by his own glorious death, a sort of priestly motive led him to dress his person in the jewelled vouchers of his own shining deeds; if thus to have adorned himself for the altar and the sacrifice were indeed vainglory, then affectation and fustian is each more heroic line in the great epics and dramas, since in such lines the poet but embodies in verse those exaltations of sentiment that a nature like Nelson, the opportunity being given, vitalizes into acts.

HERMAN MELVILLE: *Billy Budd*

SECOND WORLD WAR

Angus MacDonald has sailed in no galleons, nor for that matter written anything save this one story, *Ordeal*. He wrote it for a book of merchant seamen's adventures in the Second World War. He chanced to read an announcement of this in the journal of the Seafarers' Education Service. Maybe he had a story, he thought, but he was no writer. So he went into the library of the S.E.S. at Liverpool, spoke to the librarian, and sat down forthwith and wrote. The librarian helped a little with the punctuation.

Here is what he wrote:

Ordeal

The ship I served on board, the Ellerman Liner *City of Cairo,* left Bombay on the 2nd of October, 1942, homeward bound with a crew of Europeans and lascars and a hundred passengers. At 8.30 p.m. on the 6th of November, five days after leaving Cape Town, she was torpedoed by a German submarine. Three passengers and eighteen members of the crew were killed by the explosion of the torpedoes or went down with the ship.

I was a quartermaster and had charge of No. 4 lifeboat. After seeing everything in order there and the boat lowered, I went over to the starboard side of the ship to where my mate, quartermaster Bob Ironside, was having difficulty in lowering his boat. I climbed inside the boat to clear a rope fouling the lowering gear, and was standing in the boat pushing it clear of the ship's side as it was being lowered, when a second torpedo exploded right underneath and blew the boat to bits. I remember a great flash, and then felt myself flying through space, then going down and down. When I came to I was floating in the water, and could see all sorts of wreckage around me in the dark. I could not get the light on my life-jacket to work, so I swam towards the largest bit of wreckage I could see in the darkness. This turned out to be No. 1 lifeboat and it was nearly submerged, it having been damaged by the second explosion. There were a few people clinging to the gunwale, which was down to water-level, and other people were sitting inside the flooded boat.

I climbed on board, and had a good look round to see if the boat was badly damaged. Some of the gear had floated away, and what was left was in a tangled mess. There were a few lascars, several women and children, and two European male passengers in the boat, and I explained to them that if some of them would go overboard and hang on to the gunwale or the wreckage near us for a few minutes we could bale out the boat and make it seaworthy. The women who were there acted immediately. They climbed outboard and, supported by the life-jackets everyone was wearing, held on to an empty tank that was floating near by. I felt very proud of these women and children. One woman (whose name, if I remember rightly, was Lady Tibbs) had three children, and the four of them were the first to swim to the tank. One young woman was left in the boat with two babies in her arms.

We men then started to bale out the water. It was a long and arduous task, as just when we had the gunwale a few inches clear, the light swell running would roll in and swamp the boat again. Eventually we managed to bale out the boat, and then we started to pick up survivors who were floating on rafts or just swimming. As we worked we could see the *City of Cairo* still afloat, but well down in the water, until we heard some one say, "There she goes". We watched her go down, stern first, her bow away up in the air, and then she went down and disappeared. There was no show of emotion, and we were all quiet. I expect the others, like myself, were wondering what would happen to us.

186

We picked up more survivors as the night wore on, and by the first light of dawn the boat was full. There were still people on the rafts we could see with the daylight, and in the distance were other lifeboats. We rowed about, picking up more people, among them Mr Sydney Britt, the chief officer, and quartermaster Bob Ironside, who was in No. 3 boat with me when the second torpedo struck. Bob's back had been injured, and one of his hands had been cut rather badly. We picked up others, then rowed to the other boats to see what decision had been made about our future. Mr Britt had, naturally, taken over command of our boat, and now he had a conference with Captain Rogerson, who was in another boat. They decided we would make for the nearest land, the island of St Helena, lying five hundred miles due north. We transferred people from boat to boat so that families could be together. Mr Britt suggested that, as our boat was in a bad way, with many leaks and a damaged rudder, and at least half its water supply lost, all the children should shift to a dry boat and a few adults take their places in our boat.

When everything was settled we set sail and started on our long voyage. Our boat was now overcrowded with fifty-four persons on board—twenty-three Europeans, including three women, and thirty-one lascars. There was not enough room for every one to sit down, so we had to take turns having a rest. The two worst injured had to lie down flat, so we made a place in the bows for Miss Taggart, a ship's stewardess, and cleared a space aft for my mate, quartermaster Bob Ironside. We did not know exactly what was wrong with Bob's back. We had a doctor in the boat, Dr Taskar, but he was in a dazed condition and not able to attend to the injured, so we bandaged them up as best we could with the first-aid materials on hand. The youngest person among us, Miss Diana Jarman, one of the ship's passengers, and only about twenty years of age, was a great help with the first aid. She could never do enough, either in attending to the sick and injured, boat work, or even actually handling the craft. She showed up some of the men in the boat, who seemed to lose heart from the beginning.

Once we were properly under way Mr Britt spoke to us all. He explained all the difficulties that lay ahead, and asked every one to pull their weight in everything to do with managing the boat, such as rowing during calm periods and keeping a look-out at night. He also explained that as we had lost nearly half our drinking water we must start right away on short rations. We could get two tablespoonfuls a day per person, one in the morning and one in the evening. He told us there were no passengers in a lifeboat, and every one would have to take turns baling as the boat was leaking very badly.

Before noon on that first day we saw our first sharks. They were enormous, and as they glided backward and forward under the boat it seemed they would hit and capsize us. They just skimmed the boat each time they passed, and they were never to leave us all the time we were in the boat.

The first night was quiet and the weather was fine, but we didn't get much rest. A good proportion of us had to remain standing for long periods, and now and then some one would fall over in their sleep. I was in the fore-part of the boat attending to the sails and the running gear, helped by Robert Watts from Reading, whom we called "Tiny" because he was a big man. He didn't know much about seamanship, as he was an aeronautical engineer, but he said to me that first day, "If you want anything done at any time just explain the job to me and I'll do it." His help was very welcome as we did not have many of the crew available for the jobs that needed to be done. From the very beginning the lascars refused to help in any way, and just lay in the bottom of the boat, sometimes in over a foot of water.

On the second day the wind increased, and we made good speed. Sometimes the boats were close together and at other times almost out of sight of each other. Our boat seemed to sail faster than the others, so Mr Britt had the idea that we might go ahead on our own. If we could sail faster than the others, and as we were leaking so badly, we should go ahead and when we got to St Helena we could send help to the others. Mr Britt had a talk with Captain Rogerson when our boats were close, and the captain said that if the mate thought that was the best plan then to go ahead. So we carried on on our own.

During the hours of darkness the wind rose stronger, and, as we could see the running gear was not in the best condition, we hove to. As it got still worse, we had to put out a sea anchor and take turns at the steering-oar to hold the boat into the seas. We had a bad night, and two or three times seas broke over the heavily laden boat and soaked us all to the skin. It was during this night that we noticed Dr Taskar was failing mentally. Every now and then he shouted, "Boy, bring me my coffee", or, "Boy, another beer". He had a rip in his trousers, and in the crowded boat during the night he cut a large piece out of the trousers of the ship's storekeeper, Frank Stobbart. I noticed the doctor with the knife and a piece of cloth in his hand. He was trying to fit the cloth over his own trousers. I pacified him and took his knife, a small silver knife with a whisky advertisement on the side. I had the same knife all through the years I was a prisoner in Germany, and only lost it after the war while serving in another Ellerman liner.

At noon on the third day the wind abated, and we set sails again and went on. We had lost sight of the other boats now and were on our own. We all expected to see a rescue ship or plane at any time, but nothing turned up. On the evening of the fourth day the doctor got worse, and rambled in his speech. He kept asking for water, and once Mr Britt gave him an extra ration, although there was not much to spare. During the night the doctor slumped over beside me, and I knew he was dead. That was the first death in the boat. We cast the body overboard at dawn while Mr Britt read a short prayer. We all felt gloomy after this first burial, and wondered who would be next.

Later in the day I crawled over to have a yarn with my mate Bob, and he said, "Do you think we have a chance, Angus?" I said, "Everything will be all right, Bob. We are bound to be picked up." Bob hadn't long been married, and he was anxious about his wife and little baby in Aberdeen. He couldn't sit up, and I was afraid his back was broken or badly damaged.

Day and night the lascars kept praying to Allah, and repeating "Pani, sahib, pani, sahib", and they would never understand that the water was precious and had to be rationed out. On the sixth morning we found three of them dead in the bottom of the boat. The old engine-room serang read a prayer for them, and Tiny and I pushed them overboard, as the lascars never would help to bury their dead. The only two natives who helped us at any time were the old serang, a proper gentleman, and a fireman from Zanzibar, and they couldn't do enough to help.

We were getting flat calms for long periods, and we lowered the sails and used the oars. We didn't make much headway, but the work helped to keep our minds and bodies occupied. I know that doing these necessary tasks helped to keep me physically fit and able to stand up to the ordeal that lay ahead. There were a few Europeans who never gave a helping hand, and I noticed that they were the first to fail mentally. They died in the first two weeks.

I was worried about Miss Taggart's sores, as they had now festered and we had nothing to dress them with except salt water. With her lying in the same position all the time her back was a mass of sores. Tiny knew more about first aid than the rest of us, and with the aid of old lifejackets he padded her up a bit. But on the seventh night she died and slipped down from her position in the bows. As she fell she got tangled up with another passenger, a Mr Ball from Calcutta, and when we got things straightened out they were both dead. A few more lascars died during the same night, and we had to bury them all at daybreak. The sharks were there in shoals that morning, and the water was churned up as they glided backward and forward near the bodies. Things were now getting worse on board, and a good few of the people sat all day with their heads on their chests doing and saying nothing. I talked to one young engineer, and told him to pull himself together as he was young and healthy and to take a lesson from Diana, who was always cheerful and bright. She had told us, "Please don't call me Miss Jarman; just call me Diana." The young engineer did pull himself back to normal but within two days he dropped back and gave up hope and died. As we buried the bodies the boat gradually became lighter and the worst leaks rose above the water-line, so there was not so much water to bale out, although we had still to bale day and night.

Our own ship's stewardess, Annie Crouch, died on the tenth day. She had been failing mentally and physically for a time, and persisted in sitting in the bottom of the boat. We shifted her to drier places, but she always slid back. Her feet and legs had swollen enormously. Her death left only one woman among us, Diana. She was still active and full of life, and she spent most of her time at the tiller. Mr Britt was beginning to show signs of mental strain, and often mumbled to himself. If I asked him a question he would answer in a dazed sort of way. I worried about him a lot, for he was always a gentleman, and every one thought the world of him. On the twelfth day he was unable to sit up or talk, so we laid him down alongside Bob Ironside, who was also failing fast. Bob called me over one day, and asked me if I thought there was still a chance. I said certainly there was, and urged him not to give up hope as he would soon be home. He said, "I can't hang on much longer, Angus. When I die, will you take off my ring and send it home if you ever get back?" There were only a few able-bodied men left among the Europeans now, and Tiny Watts, my right-hand man, died on the fourteenth morning. He hadn't complained at any time, and I was surprised when I found him dead. We buried seven bodies that morning: five lascars, Tiny, and Frank Stobbart. It took a long time to get them overboard, and I had to lie down and rest during the operation.

On the fifteenth morning at dawn both Mr Britt and Bob were dead, also three other Europeans, and a few lascars. A few more lascars died during the day. One of the firemen said that if he couldn't get extra water he would jump overboard, and later in the day he jumped over the stern. He had forgotten to take off his life-jacket, and as we were now too weak to turn the boat round to save him, the sharks got him before he could drown. The remaining survivors voted that I should take over command. On looking through Mr Britt's papers I could see the estimated distances for each day up to about the tenth day, but after that there were only scrawls and scribbles. When I checked up on the water I found we had enough only for a few days, so I suggested cutting down the issue to one tablespoonful a day. There were plenty of biscuits and malted-milk tablets, but without water to moisten the mouth the biscuits only went into a powder and fell out of the corner of the mouth again. Those people with false teeth had still more trouble as the malted-milk tablets went into a doughy mess and stuck to their teeth.

The boat was now much drier, and there was not so much baling to do as we rode higher in the water and most of the leaks were above the surface. The movement, however, was not so steady as when we were heavier laden, but about the middle of the seventeenth night the boat appeared to become very steady again. I heard Diana cry out, "We're full of water", and I jumped up and found the boat half-full of water. I could see the plug hole glittering like a blue light, and I started looking for the plug. I put a spare one in place, and a few of us baled out the water. There were two people lying near the plug-hole, and they seemed to take no interest in what was happening. About an hour later I discovered the plug gone again and water entering the boat. I put the plug back, and this time I lay down with an eye on watch. Sure enough, in less than half an hour I saw a hand over the plug pulling it out. I grasped the hand and found it belonged to a young European. He was not in his right mind, although he knew what he was doing. When I asked him why he tried to sink the boat he said, "I'm going to die, so we might as well go together." I shifted him to the fore part of the boat, and we others took turns in keeping an eye on him, but he managed to destroy all the contents of the first-aid box and throw them over the side. He died the next day, with seven or eight lascars, and a banker from Edinburgh, a Mr Crichton. Mr Crichton had a patent waistcoat fitted with small pockets, and the valuables we found there we put with rings and other things in Diana's handbag. Among

Mr Crichton's possessions were the three wise monkeys in jade and a silver brandy flask that was empty.

At the end of the third week there were only eight of us left alive in the boat: the old engine-room serang, the fireman from Zanzibar, myself, Diana, Jack Edmead, the steward, Joe Green from Wigan, Jack Oakie from Birmingham, and a friend of his, Jack Little. Two of them had been engineers working on the new Howrah bridge at Calcutta.

There was still no rain, we had not had a single shower since we started our boat voyage, and the water was nearly finished. Only a few drops were left on the bottom of the tank. About the middle of the fourth week I was lying down dozing in the middle of the night when the boat started to rattle and shake. I jumped up, thinking we had grounded on an island. Then I discovered a large fish had jumped into the boat and was thrashing about wildly. I grabbed an axe that was lying handy, and hit the fish a few hard cracks. The axe bounded off it like rubber, and it was a while before I made any impression, but when it did quieten down I tied a piece of rope round the tail and hung the fish on the mast. It took me all my time to lift the fish, as it was about three feet long and quite heavy. I lay down again, and at daybreak examined the fish closer. It was a dog-fish. During the struggle with it I had gashed a finger against its teeth, and as we now had no bandages or medicine all I could do was wash the cut in sea water before I proceeded to cut up the fish. I had heard and read about people drinking blood, and I thought that I could get some blood from the carcase for drinking. I had a tough job cutting up the fish with my knife, and only managed to get a few teaspoonfuls of dirty, reddish-black blood. I cut the liver and heart out, and sliced some of the flesh off. By this time all hands were awake, although every one was feeling weak. I gave the first spoonful of blood to Diana to taste, but she spat it out and said it was horrible. I tried every one with a taste, but nobody could swallow the vile stuff. I tried it myself, but couldn't get it down. It seemed to swell the tongue. We tried eating the fish, but that was also a failure. I chewed and chewed at my piece, but couldn't swallow any and eventually spat it into the sea.

The day following my encounter with the big dog-fish my hand and arm swelled up, and Diana said I had blood poisoning. The following day it was much worse, and throbbed painfully. I asked Diana if she could do anything for it, as we had no medical supplies left. She advised me to let the hand drag in the water, and later in the day she squeezed the sore, and all sorts of matter came out. I then put my hand back in the water, and that seemed to draw out more poison. At intervals Diana squeezed the arm from the shoulder downward, and gradually got rid of the swelling, although the sore didn't heal for months, and the scar remains to this day.

There was no water left now, and Jack Oakie, Jack Little, and the Zanzibar fireman all died during the one night. It took the remainder of us nearly a whole day to lift them from the bottom of the boat and roll them overboard. The serang was now unconscious and Joe Green was rambling in his speech. There were a few low clouds drifting over us, but no sign of rain, and I had lost count of the days. I had written up Mr Britt's log-book to the end of the fourth week, but after that day and night seemed to be all the same. Diana had the sickness that nearly every one in turn had suffered: a sore throat and a thick yellow phlegm oozing from the mouth. I think it was due to us lying in the dampness all the time and never getting properly dry. The sails were now down and spread across the boat as I was too feeble to do anything in the way of running the boat. Against all advice, I often threw small quantities of sea water down my throat, and it didn't seem to make me any worse, although I never overdid it.

One night Joe Green would not lie in the bottom of the boat in comfort, but lay on the after end in an uncomfortable position. When I tried to get him to lie down with us he said, "I won't last out the night, and if I lie down there you will never be able to lift me up and get me over the side." The next morning he was dead. So was the serang. Two grand old men, though of different races. There were only three of us left now. Jack Edmead was pretty bad by now, and Diana still had the sore throat. But we managed to get the bodies over the side. The serang by this time was very thin and wasted, and if he had been any heavier we would not have managed to get him over.

By this time we were only drifting about on the ocean. I had put the jib up a couple of times, but discovered we drifted in circles, so I took it down again. One day I had a very clear dream as I lay there in the bottom of the boat. I dreamed that the three of us were walking up the pierhead at Liverpool, and the dream was so clear that I really believed it would happen. I told Diana and Jack about the dream, and said I was sure we would be picked up. There wasn't a drop of water in the boat now, and the three of us just lay there dreaming of water in all sorts of ways. Sometimes it was about a stream that ran past our house when I was a child, another time I would be holding a hose

193

and spraying water all round, but it was always about water. Jack was getting worse, and was laid out in the stern, while Diana was forward where it was drier. Sick as she was, she always used to smile and say, "We still have a chance if we could only get some rain."

Then one night rain came. I was lying down half asleep when I felt the rain falling on my face. I jumped up shouting, "Rain, rain", but Jack wasn't able to get up and help me. Diana was in pretty bad condition, but she managed to crawl along and help me spread the main sail to catch the water. It was a short sharp shower and didn't last long, but we collected a few pints in the sail and odd corners of the boat. We didn't waste a drop, and after pouring it carefully into the tank we sucked the raindrops from the woodwork and everywhere possible. Diana had trouble swallowing anything as her throat was swollen and raw, but I mixed some pemmican with water, and we had a few spoonfuls each. The water was very bitter as the sail had been soaked in salt water for weeks, but it tasted good to us. We all felt better after our drink, and I sat down in the well of the boat that day and poured can after can of sea water over myself, and gave Diana a bit of a wash. She was in good spirits now, although she could only speak in whispers. She told me about her home in the south of England: I think she said it was Windsor, on the Thames. She was very fond of horses and tennis and other sports, and she said, "You must come and visit us when we get home," which showed that like myself she had a firm conviction that we would get picked up.

The three days after the rain were uneventful. Diana was a bit better, but Jack was in a bad way, and lying down in the stern end. On the third day I had another shower-bath sitting down in the boat, as it had livened me up a lot the last time. Afterwards I set the jib and tried to handle the main sail, but couldn't make it, so I spread the sail and used it as a bed. I had the best sleep in weeks. In the early hours of the morning Diana shook me, and said excitedly, "Can you hear a plane?" I listened, and heard what sounded like a plane in the distance, so I dashed aft and grabbed one of the red flares and tried to light it. It didn't go off, so I struck one of the lifeboat matches. It ignited at once, and I held it up as high as I could, and immediately a voice shouted, "All right, put that light out." It was still dark, but on looking in the direction of the voice we could see the dim outline of a ship, and hear the sound of her diesel engines. The same voice shouted, "Can you come alongside?" God knows how we managed, but manage it we did. Even Jack found enough strength to give a hand, and with Diana at the tiller he and I rowed the boat alongside the ship. A line was thrown to us, and I made it fast. A pilot ladder was dropped, and two men came down to help us on board. They tied a rope round Diana, and with the help of others on the ship hauled her on board. I climbed up unaided, and the men helped Jack. The first thing I asked for was a drink, and we sat on a hatch waiting to see what would happen. We thought we were on a Swedish ship at first, but I saw a Dutch flag painted across the hatch. Then I heard a couple of men talking, and I knew then we were on a German ship, as I had a slight knowledge of the language. I told the other two, and Diana said, "It doesn't matter what nationality it is as long as it is a ship."

A man came to us soon and asked us to go with him and meet the captain. Two of the crew helped Diana and Jack, and we were taken amidships to the doctor's room, where a couch had been prepared for Diana. The captain arrived, and asked us about our trip in the boat and inquired how long we had been in it. I told him our ship had been torpedoed on the 6th of November, and that I had lost count of the days. He said this was the 12th of December, and that we were on board the German ship *Rhakotis,* and we should be well looked after. I remembered the bag of valuables in the boat, and told the captain where Diana's bag was. The bag was found and passed up, and given into the captain's charge. It was probably lost when the ship was sunk three weeks later. The lifeboat was stripped and sunk before the ship got under way again.

We were given cups of coffee, but were told that the doctor's orders were for us not to drink much at a time, and only eat or drink what he ordered. Diana was lying on the doctor's couch, and when the three of us were left alone for a while she bounced up and down on the springs and said, "This is better than lying in that wet boat." Later Jack and I were given a hot bath by a medical attendant, and my hand was bandaged, as it was still festering. We were taken aft to a cabin, and Diana was left in the doctor's room. The crew had orders not to bother us and to leave us on our own, as we had to rest as much as possible. When I looked at myself in the mirror I didn't recognize myself with a red beard and haggard appearance. There didn't seem to be any flesh left on my body, only a bag of bones. Jack looked even worse with his black beard and hollow cheeks.

We had been given some tablets and injected, and were now

195

told to go to bed. Before I did so I asked one of the crew to fetch me a bottle of water. Although this was against the doctor's orders the man did so, and I hid the bottle under my pillow. Then I asked another man to bring me a bottle of water, and in this way I collected a few bottles and I drank the lot. Jack was already asleep when I turned in after drinking the water, and I turned in on the bunk above him. We slept for hours and when I awoke I found I had soaked the bedding. Later I discovered I had soaked Jack's bed too. He was still asleep. I wakened him and apologized, but he only laughed. The steward brought us coffee at 7 a.m., and when I told him about my bladder weakness he didn't seem annoyed, but took the bedclothes away to be changed. It was a year before I was able to hold any liquid for more than an hour or so.

We were well looked after and well fed on the German ship, and from the first day I walked round the decks as I liked. Jack was confined to bed for a few days. We were not allowed to visit Diana, but the captain came aft and gave us any news concerning her. She couldn't swallow any food, and was being fed by injections. When we had been five days on the ship the doctor and the captain came along to our cabin, and I could see they were worried. The captain did the talking, and said that as the English girl still hadn't been able to eat, and couldn't go on living on injections, the doctor wanted to operate on her throat and clear the inflammation. But first of all he wanted our permission. I had never liked the doctor and had discovered he was disliked by nearly every one on board, but still, he was the doctor, and should know more about what was good for Diana than I could. So I told the captain that if the doctor thought it was necessary to operate he had my permission as I wanted to see Diana well again. Jack said almost the same, and the captain asked if we would like to see her. We jumped at the chance, and went with the doctor. She seemed quite happy, and looked well, except for being thin. Her hair had been washed and set, and she said she was being well looked after. We never mentioned the operation to her, but noticed she could still talk only in whispers.

That evening at seven o'clock the captain came to us, and I could see that something was wrong. He said, "I have bad news for you. The English girl has died. Will you follow me, please?" We went along, neither of us able to say a word. We were taken to the doctor's room where she lay with a bandage round her throat. You would never know she was dead, she looked so peaceful. The doctor spoke, and said in broken English that the operation was a success, but the girl's heart was not strong enough to stand the anaesthetic. I couldn't speak, and turned away broken-hearted. Jack and I went aft again, and I turned into my bunk and lay crying like a baby nearly all night. It was the first time I had broken down and cried, and I think Jack was the same. The funeral was the next day, and when the time came we went along to the fore-deck where the ship's crew were all lined up wearing uniform and the body was in a coffin covered by the Union Jack. The captain made a speech in German, and then spoke in English for our benefit. There were tears in the eyes of many of the Germans, as they had all taken an interest in the English girl. The ship was stopped, and after the captain had said a prayer, the coffin slid slowly down the slipway into the sea. It had been weighted, and sank slowly. The crew stood to attention bareheaded until the coffin disappeared. It was an impressive scene, and a gallant end to a brave and noble girl. We had been through so much together, and I knew I would never forget her.

The *Rhakotis* was bound for Bordeaux, and was due there about New Year's Day. We had a good Christmas at sea, with all sorts of food, and as I had regained my normal appetite by then I was able to take my share of everything. The butcher had killed two pigs, and we had as much roast pork as we could eat, I am sure we got a better Christmas as prisoners on the *Rhakotis* than many seamen had on British ships.

There was great excitement on board on the 31st of December, and word got round that we had a rendezvous with four U-boats who would escort us into port. We stopped at 7 p.m. that evening, and within a few minutes the subs came close alongside out of the darkness. Nobody stopped us looking over the side at them, and we saw a couple of officers come aboard and meet the captain. They didn't stay long, and within half an hour we were on our way again. The subs disappeared, but they must have been some-where in the vicinity. At 4 a.m. on New Year's Day Jack woke me up and said, "Look at the yellow light out on deck." The whole ship was lit up, and when I went outside I saw a flare floating above the ship. Then I heard the drone of a plane, and the anti-aircraft guns opened up. The plane dropped a load of incendiaries and some bombs. A few incendiaries landed on the ship amidships, but I don't think they did much damage. After a time all went quiet again, and we turned in. Jack remarked that this was a good beginning to the New Year.

We were having a special dinner that afternoon at 4.30 p.m., when I heard an explosion I guessed was gunfire. Immediately loud alarm bells sounded, and armed guards appeared at the door. I asked one of them what was the matter, and he said simply, "English cruiser". We could hear the gunfire plainer now, and then we felt the ship being hit. The noise was terrific, and there were loud crashes not far from where we waited. An armed guard ran down the alleyway calling out, "To the boats". Others were unwinding a coil of electric flex and setting a box against the ship's side. This was a time-bomb to scuttle the ship after we got clear, but it was not required as the ship was on fire all over and badly damaged by direct hits. I didn't know from which side the shells were coming, so I picked the port-side boat, and no sooner got there than I saw the British cruiser a good way off on the port side. She was firing salvoes, and I could see the flashes and hear the shells screaming past. The weather was bad at the time, and a large swell was running, so it wasn't easy getting the boats away. I slid down a life-line into the boat, and was no sooner in it than a large sea came along and partly submerged the boat. I had nothing to do with the handling of the boat as the Germans were all at their proper stations, but I helped to push it clear with a boathook. We were just clear when there was a shout from the *Rhakotis,* and we could see two men waving and shouting for us to come back. The ship had a big list, and was a mass of flames from stem to stern, but the boat was turned back, and the two men jumped into the water, and were dragged into the boat. Shells were exploding all around, and I expected any minute the boat would be hit. The cruiser kept firing until the *Rhakotis* was on her beam ends, then turned and went full speed away. She must have known there were U-boats in the vicinity. I was very disappointed, as I was so sure they would have picked us up. As their ship rolled over and went down slowly the Germans took off their caps and gave her three cheers.

We were now alone in the Bay of Biscay, and in darkness. The starboard boat was not in sight, and it was many years before I learned that Jack Edmead was in her, and that she managed to reach Spain. From there poor Jack was sent home, only to join a ship that was later torpedoed. There were thirty-five of us in the port boat, including a few prisoners. I was the only Britisher. Sitting beside me were two young Danish boys, only fifteen years of age, whose ship had been captured in the Indian Ocean. These boys had been good to Jack and me on the German ship, and they turned up at the prisoner-of-war camp where I was placed. After their release they sent me a few welcome parcels of food.

The boat was in good condition and well stocked with water and large biscuits. Although there was a tremendous sea running, she was fairly steady, and only once or twice did she take any water on board during that wild night. I had no hat on, and as it was New Year's Day and cold I looked round for something to put on my head. I could see a beret sticking out of one of the German's pockets, so I quietly drew it out and put it on. He was wearing a sou-wester and did not miss the beret.

The following morning the wind had died down a bit, but there was still a big sea running. The officer in charge took a chance and set sail for the nearest land on the French coast. We each had a handful of biscuits and a glass of water for breakfast, and we were quite happy. About eleven o'clock some one shouted out "U-boat", and I could see the periscope coming up out of the water close to us. The conning-tower appeared, and then the sub itself showed up. The hatch opened, and the commander shouted to the officer in charge of our boat, giving instructions on how we were to transfer to the submarine. We took the boat as close as we dared without touching the sub, as bumping would have capsized us, and as the nose of the sub rose to the sea one man at a time grabbed a wire and was pulled on board. It took a long time to get us all transferred, and once on the sub we all threw our life-jackets away and went below. It was only a small submarine, returning to port after fourteen days hunting the Atlantic convoys when it was ordered by radio to find the two boats from the *Rhakotis*. As soon as we got below each man was given a large mug of steaming coffee laced with rum, then shown to a spot where he had to lie. The submarine was cramped enough with its own crew, and now with thirty-five extra men it was like a sardine-tin.

We were only submerged fifteen minutes when a harsh alarm bell rang, and the nose of the sub dipped as she crash-dived. A few seconds later there were three tremendous explosions. The first shook us, the second was worse, and the third must have been very close, for the whole sub shook, and we were thrown about. I fell off the bunk I shared with another man and landed on the two spare torpedoes on the deck. The engines were stopped, and we were ordered not to speak or move. The sub was now on an even keel, and there didn't seem to be anything seriously wrong. Later we were to learn that a British plane on anti-submarine patrol had sighted us from a distance, and dropped depth-charges over the spot where we had been. After lying motionless for about an hour the engines throbbed again, and we went on our way. One of the crew told me we were bound for Bordeaux.

The air was getting very foul, and we were told that as we wouldn't surface until after dark we must lie still and keep quiet, as the air was used up by unnecessary movement. We had a good meal of bread, cheese, and coffee during the afternoon, and then lay down to await night and fresh air. During the afternoon a voice speaking English came through the loudspeaker, saying that anyone caught touching any of the machinery would be thrown overboard. As I had no wish to stay longer in the submarine than I had to, I had no intention of doing it any damage. The order to keep still was very hard on me as my bladder was still very weak, so I asked one of the officers if I could speak to the commander. On explaining my predicament he took me amidships, and I had a talk with the commander. He was only about twenty-five, though he was the oldest member of the ship's company, and he, like the rest of the crew, had a beard. He spoke perfect English, and had a talk with me about the trip in the boat. He told me that as Bordeaux was blockaded by British planes he had decided to carry on to Saint-Nazaire, and we should be there in a couple of days. He said that as the midships portion of the submarine was too crowded to let me relieve myself he would give me a case of empty beer bottles to use.

We surfaced soon after this, and we could hear the mechanism of the sub working as we rose. After assuring themselves that the coast was clear the Germans opened up the conning-tower, and fresh air poured in. Air was pumped all through the vessel, and the diesel engine started up and kept going until nearly day-break. The cook set his fire going, and made a hot meal for all hands, which he couldn't do when the sub was submerged. It was much more comfortable now with the fresh air, and every one was happy and looking forward to going on shore. In the early morning we submerged again, and the submarine ran on batteries. It wasn't too bad, as occasionally, if the coast was clear, the commander would surface for short periods, and we could get fresh air.

About noon on the third day of January the warning bell went again, and the Germans dashed to their stations. I was lying alongside the spare torpedoes and quite close to the torpedo-tubes, and could watch the men waiting for orders. The sub would rise a few inches at a time, then submerge a bit, and it sounded just like being in a lift on shore. This went on for a while, and I asked one of the Germans what was going on. He said it was a British destroyer. You can imagine how I felt lying there and knowing we were stalking one of our own destroyers. Everything was deadly quiet, and then all of a sudden the alarm bell clanged out harshly. Immediately the nose of the sub went down at a terrific speed as she crash-dived. She seemed to be standing on her head. The suspense was terrible, and I could see that even the men standing by the torpedo-tubes were looking a bit drawn, as though waiting for something. Then came the first depth-charge, and the sub shook with the force of the explosion. We were still going down, but the angle was not so steep, and gradually the submarine came to an even keel. Then came the second and third explosions, and we were thrown all over the place. The sub seemed to jump and then rolled from side to side. The lights went out, and all the escape hatches were closed. She seemed to bump a bit a few seconds later, and I could only guess that we had hit the sea bottom. We could hear depth-charges going off, but they seemed to be farther away each time. There wasn't a sound now in our compartment, and I thought to myself that after coming through what I had I was to finish up like this, suffocating in a submarine at the bottom of the sea. A voice in the darkness told us to lie still and not move from where we were, which was rather hard to obey as we were all lying over each other. I lay across the spare torpedoes with a big German lying on my legs. Nobody in our compartment knew what damage had been done, but no water was coming in at our end. No orders were coming through, so we could only guess something had gone wrong amidships or aft. We lay for hours, the air getting foul, and drops of moisture falling on us from the deck head. I was choking and could hear the heavy breathing of others, and knew they were suffering as much as I was. The under-officer with us warned us not to speak or move as we would use up what air was left. I didn't think I should last long the way we were, and just lay feeling the drops of moisture dripping down in the darkness.

It seemed hours later when we heard a tapping from the other side of the bulkhead. Some one on our side tapped back an answer. They must have had some sort of code worked out beforehand, for the tapping went on for some time, until eventually the watertight door was opened, and one of the crew came through with a torch and some small square boxes which he placed on the deck. One of the men told me this was a way to test the condition of the air. I could hear a lot of hammering going on in the after section of the submarine, and a few men were working by torch-light on some mechanism in our compartment. It was early morning before the lights came on again, and the commander spoke through the loudspeaker and told every one to stay calm, and the damage to the after end would be repaired. We were all gasping for air, as the thirty-five extra men had used up the air sooner than would the normal crew.

The submarine got under way about daybreak and rose slowly to the surface. The hatches opened, and fresh air gushed in. We had no more incidents during the trip to Saint-Nazaire, which we reached about noon on the 4th of January. We slid slowly into the submarine pens, and the Germans all went ashore where a military band played on the quay and a number of high-ranking officers welcomed them. The remainder of us, all prisoners, stood on the deck watching everything, and wondering what was going to happen to us. Later in the afternoon I was taken on shore for interrogation, and then placed in a cell on my own. I remained there until the following day, when a guard came to take me to a truck bound for Nantes, and the train to Wilhelmshaven and captivity. I was sent to the Merchant Navy prison camp at Milag Nord, where I remained until the British Army arrived to free us in May 1945.

ANGUS MACDONALD

They that go down to the sea in ships, that do business in great
    waters;
These see the works of the Lord, and his wonders in the deep.
For he commandeth, and raiseth the stormy wind, which lifteth
    up the waves thereof.
They mount up to the heaven, they go down again to the depths:
    their soul is melted because of trouble.
They reel to and fro, and stagger like a drunken man, and are at
    their wits' end.
Then they cry unto the Lord in their trouble, and he bringeth
    them out of their distresses.
He maketh the storm a calm, so that the waves thereof are still.
Then are they glad because they be quiet; so he bringeth them
    unto their desired haven.

From PSALM CVII

ACKNOWLEDGEMENTS

Grateful acknowledgement is due to the following authors, agents and publishers for permission to include copyright material:

Angus MacDonald and George G. Harrap & Co. Ltd for the short story "Ordeal" from *Touching the Adventures of Merchantmen in the Second World War,* ed. J. Lennox Kerr (pages 185–202); J. Weston Martyr and William Blackwood & Sons Ltd for extracts from the short story *The £200 Millionaire* (pages 141–151); Jacques Chambrun Inc. and Peter Davies Ltd for an extract from *Ships and Women* by Bill Adams (pages 107–111); Captain Francis Newbolt and John Murray Ltd for the poem "Drake's Drum" from *Poems New and Old* by Sir Henry Newbolt (page 38); The Society of Authors and Dr John Masefield, O.M., for "Sea Fever" (page 36) and extracts from "Dauber" (pages 84–89); Angus & Robertson Ltd for an extract from *Slavers of the South Seas* by Thomas Dunbabin (pages 50–55); Brown, Son & Ferguson Ltd for extracts from *Last of the Windjammers* Vol. II by Basil Lubbock (pages 67 and 169–173); The Clarendon Press, Oxford, for the poem "A Passer-By" by Robert Bridges (page 37); J. M. Dent & Sons Ltd for passages from *The Nigger of the "Narcissus"* by Joseph Conrad (pages 45–48, 91–94 and 111–115); Gerald Duckworth & Co. Ltd for an extract from *The Brassbounder* by David W. Bone (pages 102–106); William Heinemann Ltd for an extract from *Castles in Spain* by John Galsworthy (page 44); The Council of the Hakluyt Society for the passage from Gomez Eannes de Zurara's *The Chronicle of the Discovery and Conquest of Guinea,* transl. and ed. C. R. Beazley and E. Prestage (pages 40–43), and for extracts from "A Report of the Trueth of the Fight About the Isles of Açores, the last of August, 1591" by Sir Walter Raleigh, as published in *Hakluyt's Principall Navigations, 1598–1600;* the Controller of Her Majesty's Stationery Office and Longmans, Green & Co. Ltd for extracts from *Naval Operations (History of the Great War* Vol. IV) by Sir Henry Newbolt (pages 167–168); Methuen & Co. Ltd for an extract from *Out of An Old Sea Chest* by Count Felix von Luckner (pages 168–169); Percival Marshall

& Co. Ltd for an extract from *Master in Sail* by James Learmont (pages 96–100); William Reed Ltd for an extract from Reed's *Seamanship and Nautical Knowledge* (pages 81–82); Seafarers' Education Service for an essay by Kenneth Hardman which first appeared in the journal *Seafarer* (pages 133–137); The Society of Authors and Dr John Masefield, O.M. for an extract from the poem "Ships" (pages 89–90).

The photograph of the Portuguese cod-fishing schooner *Ana Maria* between pages 136–137 is reproduced by kind permission of H.E. Dr Pedro Theotónio Pereira, G.C.V.O., Portuguese Ambassador in Washington.

Acknowledgement is also due to the following, who in addition to the above-mentioned have kindly given their permission to include copyright material in the American edition of this book:

The Macmillan Company for "Sea Fever" (page 36) and extracts from "The Wanderer" (page 84), "Dauber" (pages 85–89) and "Ships" (pages 89–90); Doubleday & Company, Inc. and the Trustees of the Joseph Conrad Estate for extracts from *The Nigger of the "Narcissus"* by Joseph Conrad (pages 45–48, 91–94 and 111–115); E. P. Dutton & Co. Inc. for an extract from *The Brassbounder* by David W. Bone (pages 102–106); and the Controller of Her Britannic Majesty's Stationery Office for extracts from *Naval Operations (History of the Great War Vol. IV)* by Sir Henry Newbolt (pages 167–168); Charles Scribner's Sons for an extract from *Castles in Spain* by John Galsworthy (page 44).